DAVIS CUP® by BNP PARIBAS

2011

ITF
International Tennis Federation ®

Text by Clive White

The International Tennis Federation

Universe

First published in the United States of America in 2011 by
UNIVERSE PUBLISHING
A Division of Rizzoli International Publications, Inc.
300 Park Avenue South
New York, NY 10010
www.rizzoliusa.com

© 2011 by the International Tennis Federation

2012 2013 2014 / 10 9 8 7 6 5 4 3 2 1

Designed by Domino 4 Limited, Weybridge, United Kingdom
Printed in Italy

ISBN: 978-0-7893-2197-8

CONTENTS

President's Message

It never ceases to amaze me how the very best players in the world can raise their game when competing in Davis Cup by BNP Paribas.

Nowhere was this more obvious than in the fourth rubber of this year's final between Spain and Argentina in front of 75,000 spectators over the course of the weekend at the Olympic Stadium in Seville.

Rafael Nadal, a player who has seemingly won everything there is to win, showed his true brilliance by battling back from a set and a break down against an inspired performance from Juan Martin del Potro.

Such is the esteem in which the competition is held that players are rightly passionate about competing for their country. One need only to look at the contrasting reactions of Nadal and del Potro after their memorable match to see how much winning Davis Cup means to them.

The former was overwhelmed by happiness (not to mention a few of his countrymen) while the latter was left wiping the tears from his eyes as his teammates offered words of consolation.

For del Potro, it was a particularly difficult final. The tall man from Tandil played some of the best tennis of the weekend and spent nearly nine hours on court over the course of his two rubbers, but came up short on both occasions. No-one can take anything away from him, however, for he played his part in what will be remembered as a classic Davis Cup encounter.

With contests like this it is little wonder that the competition continues to thrive. Davis Cup is the only competition that gives players the opportunity to represent their country, and 27 of the top 30 men rose to the challenge this year. That so many of the best players commit to a competition that isn't mandatory shows that although it can mean sacrifice, the rewards are high.

Spain maintained its stranglehold on the Davis Cup with a fifth title in 11 years, but with 520 players from 121 nations competing across the globe there were many more stories to be told.

Television played its part by broadcasting Davis Cup in over 180 countries, while the internet continued to prove itself the perfect portal for a competition with a worldwide reach.

The official Davis Cup websites, DavisCup.com and CopaDavis.com, recorded over 17 million page views this year and more than 350,000 people visited the live streaming site on DavisCup.tv.

Spectators are not just tuning in online, however, with almost 600,000 fans attending 81 ties this year, including a total attendance of 75,000 across the three days of the final in Seville.

I would like to extend my gratitude to BNP Paribas, who completed its tenth year of title sponsorship, and say how proud we are to have secured the bank as our title sponsor until 2016. My thanks go also to our international sponsors Turismo Madrid, HP, Rolex, Hugo Boss, Adecco and NH Hoteles, and our international partner Wilson.

All that remains is for me to thank the author of this book, Clive White, for his sterling efforts in bringing Davis Cup to life, and to congratulate the wonderful work of the photographers who have once again captured the spirit of the competition with some truly remarkable images.

I must congratulate Spain once again for another memorable Davis Cup victory and thank the National Associations that have been involved in staging the ties. I cannot wait to see what next season brings.

Francesco Ricci Bitti
ITF President

BNP PARIBAS | The bank for a changing world

The love affair continues

BNP Paribas (www.bnpparibas.com) is one of the best rated banks in the world. The Group has a presence in more than 80 countries and over 200,000 employees, including no less than 160,000 in Europe. BNP Paribas places its abilities and its skills at the service of its clients in all of the countries in which it operates. It also places them at the service of its sports sponsorship. BNP Paribas has supported tennis since 1973, demonstrating its capacity to adapt through a policy based on warm and dynamic partnership. The relationship between BNP Paribas and tennis is mutually beneficial. It has been developed with care and loyalty to the sport in order to attain a worldwide reputation that reflects the qualities of the group's work in the field of banking.

Sports sponsorship at the service of the brand

The BNP Paribas brand is a major asset for the company in its contact with people across all areas of its activity. In it they see a human quality as it conveys emotional values and above all, acts as a familiar landmark in an increasingly globalized environment. The BNP Paribas brand system is a means of reconciling a strong international image with a local relationship. BNP Paribas has now become a powerful, innovative, warm, and cohesive international brand. Tennis sponsorship is one of the springboards used to spread its influence.

Tennis sponsorship at the service of the international deployment of the brand

BNP Paribas has gradually developed its partnership mechanism to accompany all aspects of the tennis boom: professional, family, educational, and social. From the year 2000 onward, the emphasis has been placed on developing tennis partnerships on an international basis in order to support the growth of the group's banking activities throughout the world. Thus sports sponsorship became the chosen means of supporting the development of the reputation of the BNP Paribas brand in countries where the group is established. This strategic choice initially took the form of Davis Cup sponsorship, which started in 2001. Step by step the structure was reinforced with support provided for 5 ATP Masters 1000 (the BNP Paribas Masters in Paris, the Monte Carlo Masters, the Internazionali BNL d'Italia in Rome, the BNP Paribas Open in Indian Wells and the Shanghai Masters). Our digital sponsorship activity continues to strengthen too with our tennis website wearetennis.com, a home to exclusive tournament content, behind the scenes information and ticket competitions enabling even more fans to get the best seats at professional tournaments.

In the same way, the Group's values and social commitments are reflected in the further development of its sponsorship program, which includes:

• Support for women's sports through Fed Cup by BNP Paribas, the TEB BNP Paribas WTA Championships in Istanbul and the Bank of the West Classic tournament in California (WTA Tour)
• Support for underprivileged youth through the "Fête le Mur" charity (created by Yannick Noah)
• Diversity through the BNP Paribas World Team Cup and NEC Tour wheelchair events.

Our commitment is one of the longest in the history of the sport, just like the relationship the bank aims to develop every day with its clients, based on trust and reciprocity.

We are proud to be the title partner of Davis Cup and hope you will enjoy reliving the great moments of 2011 in this yearbook. We would like to congratulate all the teams that took part in the competition and in particular both the Spanish and Argentine teams for the fantastic final they played in Seville. See you in 2012!

Baudouin Prot
Chairman, BNP Paribas

Foreword

In a sport played for forty-eight weeks of the year as an individual, Davis Cup has provided me with some magical moments and a whole range of emotions, all of which are intense. The experience of being part of a team gave me the opportunity to play some of my best tennis. In these last three years, the responsibility of captaining a sensational group of tennis players has provided me with a new challenge.

At the end of the day, it has been precisely this team spirit, embodied by the quest for the silver salad bowl, that has at times made me suffer; it has been exciting and entertaining; I have had to analyze and make tough choices; and I have laughed with a group of players with whom I have had the fortune of sharing two amazing victories.

I don't have the words to express just how special these two victories were, combined with a support that has been at the heart of our collective enjoyment.

The experts say that there are six principal values behind working as a group: Respect, Professionalism, Confidence, Attitude, Communication, and Commitment. All of these have been evident in the players I have had the honor of captaining over these past years.

The incredibly talented individual never works on a team without having Respect, and this has been a constant in our group—respect for every member of the team and to each and all of our rivals. On the other hand, the technical and competitive strength of this team doesn't depend only on the players' contribution but also on those who work with them and support them during the ties.

The behavior of this group, always exemplary in their manner and camaraderie, can only be defined with one word: Professionalism. Overcoming particularly difficult challenges when you are a leader requires a combination of qualities, strategies, and above all, Confidence. This last attribute, without doubt, has been the cornerstone on which we have built all of our victories. And that confidence was there for all to see this year during the very tough quarterfinal tie against the United States in Austin, when the team overcame the worst possible conditions with their amazing Attitude—an attitude that I will never forget.

Without doubt, working as a team, fighting for one goal, and facing difficult situations both mentally and physically in a professional calendar that is very tiring, has only been possible thanks to Commitment. Another aspect that has especially excited me in the last few years is the feeling of support that is understood in the values of this group. Aside from promoting winning, Spanish tennis has Communicated clearly the image that united we are stronger. Spanish tennis, through the Davis Cup, has been able to show this positive image not only in our own country, but we have also exported this idea around the world as a sign of the values that our parents instilled in us when they introduced us to sport.

I feel privileged to have been part of this group that has worked with these values to find our common goal. The record books will show our victories etched onto the plaques on the Davis Cup trophy, but I am left with an inner richness that this group has given me and that we have achieved together.

Albert Costa

One step closer to greatness

As exciting and deserved as Serbia's success was in the 2010 competition, there was no disputing which was still the best team in the world, as Spain's six-thousand-point margin over the new champion at the end of the year indicated. It was a bit like when Joe Frazier was heavyweight champion of the world and there was a fellow called Muhammad Ali still around. Spain, however, didn't have to put up with the tag of "People's Champion" for long and duly regained its official title after a one-year cessation, in Seville.

In becoming champion for the fifth time since the start of the millennium, Albert Costa's team has quickly established a reputation that bears favorable comparison with many of the great Davis Cup teams stretching back to the Four Musketeers of the late 1920s. Of course, comparisons are invidious, but the Spanish team has dominated the present era every bit as emphatically as the great French, Australian, American, and Swedish teams dominated theirs, and, like them, they have won the title on more than one surface.

Australia's domination of the event from 1950 to 1967, during which time they won the Dwight Davis trophy fifteen times, will probably never be equalled, but it is only fair to compare Spain's record with that of the countries which have competed in Davis Cup post 1971, when the Challenge Round was abolished. Since then the United States has had the best run of success, winning the trophy in four out of five years between 1978 and 1982. Coming next with a run of three titles in four years are Spain from 2008 to 2011 and Sweden from 1984 to 1987.

The Achilles' heel of that American side, spearheaded by that great Davis Cup advocate John McEnroe, was, of course, clay—Spain's strength—and in 1980 its run was broken when Guillermo Vilas and company beat them 4–1 in Buenos Aires in an Americas Inter-Zonal Final (Ivan Lendl's Czechoslovakian team went on to win the trophy that year). Spain's weaknesses are less obvious. When asked to deliver in the 2008 final on a different surface—also in Argentina—the Spanish team was equal to the task, even without its No. 1 player, Rafael Nadal.

Even the greatest tennis nations haven't always been able to handle such demands. When Harry Hopman's Australian team attempted to maintain its supremacy in the early 1960s without the great Rod Laver, it was beaten—at home—by the United States in 1963. And, of course, some countries, like Sweden, had the luxury of calling on the services of multiple Grand Slam champions in Stefan Edberg and Mats Wilander. Similarly, for a short while, Germany had two great champions in Boris Becker and Michael Stich.

In bygone days, even a good Spanish team was compromised on any surface that wasn't red. That situation has steadily changed in recent years. Carlos Moya and Juan Carlos Ferrero, although clay-court specialists, could both perform adequately on hard courts; Ferrero was a US Open finalist in 2003. But with the arrival of Nadal they have become pretty comfortable on all surfaces—even grass, which in Manuel Santana's time was famously fit "just for cows." Now we have a Spaniard who is a multiple Wimbledon champion, as well as Feliciano Lopez who has gone as far as the quarterfinals.

Although compared to the likes of McEnroe and Goran Ivanisevic—never mind Nicola Pietrangeli, who played in a record 164 rubbers all told—Nadal is a relative novice in terms of Davis Cup experience. His singles record, as it stands, is quite exceptional: twenty consecutive wins—fifteen in straight sets—and just one defeat, on his debut, as a seventeen-year-old (against Czech Republic's Jiri Novak). Only the records of Becker and Bjorn Borg, with thirty-eight and thirty-seven wins, respectively, and both with three defeats, can compare in modern times.

Spain may now be entering a less successful period in its history, but long-term its prospects in the competition still look good. During the next decade the Spanish surely have it within their powers to overtake Sweden, who are on seven wins, and possibly Great Britain and France, who have nine. The United States (with thirty-two titles) and Australia (with twenty-eight) must be the targets of a distant Spanish generation, when Nadal and company are in their dotage.

Although the Mallorcan and David Ferrer have ruled themselves out of Davis Cup play in 2012 because they want to concentrate on the Olympics, few would bet against them returning sometime soon, so strong is their love of the competition, as was clear in

Seville. But even without these two mainstays of Costa's team, Spain should remain a force, providing Fernando Verdasco can rediscover his verve and Lopez can continue in the way he has these past couple of years. Whatever doubts there may be about them as a doubles pairing, as singles players they are top drawer. And they still have people who are capable of winning World Group rubbers, like former French Open champion Ferrero.

Their depth in talent has been the envy of the world—including even France. What other country in the world could afford to have a player in the Top 10 who doesn't qualify for its Davis Cup team as Spain has in Nicolas Almagro? That, of course, may now change. At the time of writing Spain has ten players in or around the Top 50, and most of them are still young and eager for international honors. As Nadal said in Seville, "It's not that it's the end of a cycle. There are lots of good people coming, lots of people who can replace us, people who are better than us, and they can get better."

The idea that those coming up can be better than Nadal and Ferrer takes some believing, but if anyone can produce them, it's Spain. Marcel Granollers, nominally a doubles player in Davis Cup, has been steadily climbing the rankings. He finished the year with an all-time-high singles berth of No. 27 after winning his second ATP singles title in the space of four months in Valencia in November.

The Spanish team's path to the final wasn't an easy one. They started with two away ties, the second of which was strewn with pitfalls, including the absence of Nadal. The United States, their opponents, on the other hand, chose a team that couldn't have been stronger: two Top 10 singles players in Andy Roddick and Mardy Fish, and arguably the world's best doubles team in the Bryan twins. With the match played on a fast court in Roddick's hometown of Austin, Texas, you could say just about every conceivable factor was in the Americans' favor, and yet still Spain came out on top and without recourse to a fifth rubber. There probably wasn't another team in the world that could have managed that.

France was expected to provide stiffer resistance in the semifinals since Gilles Simon, Richard Gasquet, and, to a lesser extent, Jo-Wilfried Tsonga could all play on clay. In the event, they were each thrashed in straight sets. Guy Forget, the French captain, has been around long enough in Davis Cup to have seen that one coming and had even described Spain before a ball had been struck as "the best team in the world—by far."

The previous year Argentina had defied the odds by reaching the semifinals, having survived difficult away ties against Sweden and Russia, but France was a trip too far, and in keeping with Spain, the Argentines suffered a whitewash at the hands of Forget's side. In 2011 they had much better luck with the draw, although home ties against Romania and Kazakhstan could hardly have been ideal preparation for a semifinal examination in Belgrade against the defending champion.

As it happened they got a little lucky, because world No. 1 Novak Djokovic chose to go that extra yard at the US Open, which left him totally ill-prepared physically and mentally for the demands of a Davis Cup semifinal, even if Nadal managed to get himself together in time in Cordoba. Reading the situation perfectly, Tito Vazquez, the Argentine captain, decided to play both his big cards on day one—Juan Martin del Potro and David Nalbandian—and was rewarded with a 2–0 lead that looked like it wouldn't be surrendered.

If any country today deserves to win the Davis Cup it is Argentina. Four times it has reached the final and four times it has gone home empty-handed. During the last decade it has produced numerous players of extraordinary talent who are worthy heirs of the great Vilas and who, unlike the great man, can perhaps perform on both clay and hard courts, and occasionally even grass.

Argentina's hopes of success in the near future—and maximizing the exciting potential of del Potro, who showed in the final that he is almost back to his best—could rest on Nalbandian, its 2002 Wimbledon finalist, who was approaching thirty at the end of the season. His ability to remain injury-free and fit could be of paramount importance. The Argentines even have the blessing of Nadal, a great friend of theirs, who, giving a clear indication of his plans for the future, said before the final in Seville, "I hope that they don't win this one if possible, please. They can win next year." ●

First Round 4–6 March

France defeated Austria 3–2   VIENNA, AUSTRIA—INDOOR CLAY

Serbia defeated India 4–1   NOVI SAD, SERBIA—INDOOR HARD

Sweden defeated Russia 3–2   BORAS, SWEDEN—INDOOR HARD

USA defeated Chile 4–1   SANTIAGO, CHILE—OUTDOOR CLAY

Spain defeated Belgium 4–1   CHARLEROI, BELGIUM—INDOOR HARD

Kazakhstan defeated Czech Republic 3–2   OSTRAVA, CZECH REPUBLIC—INDOOR HARD

Germany defeated Croatia 3–2   ZAGREB, CROATIA—INDOOR HARD

Argentina defeated Romania 4–1   BUENOS AIRES, ARGENTINA—OUTDOOR CLAY

Introduction

Players may come and players may go, but few stay away from Davis Cup forever. We knew the absence of Novak Djokovic, the hero of the previous year's competition, at the start of the 2011 season was only temporary. He would be back—providing Serbia won, of course—like world No. 1 Rafael Nadal was after injury. Andy Roddick came out of a year-long retirement to play Davis Cup again, while his captain, Jim Courier, was back in the old routine after twelve years away.

If that wasn't enough, the World Group first-round ties provided enough excitement to fill an entire season. No sooner had Roddick returned than he saw his serve—which set a world record in a Davis Cup tie in Belarus seven years earlier—bettered by Ivo Karlovic. The giant Croatian thundered down a 251 kmph (155.96 mph) serve and still lost his rubber—and the tie—against Germany.

Joachim Johansson, returning to the game, if only momentarily, after a history of injuries, would have sympathized. It may be recalled that he once served a world-record fifty-one aces and still lost his match against Andre Agassi. This time, against Russia's Teymuraz Gabashvili, he only served thirty-three and won his rubber as the Swedes wrapped up the tie inside the first two days.

A cup competition in any sport isn't a cup competition if it doesn't throw in the odd surprise result or two. The previous year Kazakhstan took on the role of giant killer when it slayed Switzerland 5–0, and in 2011 the new Soviet Republic did it again, when it brought down arguably an even greater goliath in Czech Republic, the world No. 3, away from home.

Otherwise, the favorites—Serbia, Spain, France, United States, Sweden, and Argentina—all went safely through to the next round. The first round was newsworthy for one final reason: a tennis match taking place inside an aircraft hangar. It was a novel idea by the Austrian Tennis Federation for the purpose, obviously, of putting France to flight. But it backfired on them because, to paraphrase the slogan of another well-known Austrian enterprise, it gave the opposition wings instead. ●

Pictured below:
Martin Fischer (AUT)
is consoled by his team;
Jurgen Melzer (AUT)

Austria v France

There were more aeronautical puns flying around than planes at Vienna Airport when Austria hosted France at one of the more imaginative venue choices for a Davis Cup tie: an aircraft hangar. When the opening two rubbers both went France's way it seemed that the location had merely facilitated a quick getaway for the visitors, but as it turned out they saw rather more of the departure lounge than they would have wished.

The worlds of international airports, tennis, and motor racing have long been loosely connected, and here they all seemed to come neatly together as Niki Lauda, the former motor racing world champion and the owner of Niki Airlines, made Hangar 3 at Schwechat available to the Austrian Tennis Federation.

It followed an approach by Ronnie Leitgeb, an Austrian tennis impresario who also happens to be the manager of the country's No. 1, Jurgen Melzer. It was just a pity for Melzer and Austria that his tennis wasn't similarly inventive. In fact, it was nothing short of inexplicable that the world No. 10, who had just enjoyed his best year ever, should lose in straight sets

G. SIMON   J. CHARDY   J. BENNETEAU

MAGIQUE !

MAGIQUE !

Pictured above:

The French team;

French fans

to Jeremy Chardy, whose greatest claim to fame was that he once won Junior Wimbledon.

In such situations there is a tendency to look at what went wrong rather than what went right, but that would be doing a disservice both to the unlikely hero of this tie and his captain, Guy Forget, whose role in it cannot be underestimated.

With or without Melzer at his best, this was always going to be a tricky tie for the nine-time champions. France was without arguably its three best players: Jo-Wilfried Tsonga, Gael Monfils, and Richard Gasquet. And if there is any doubt about whether Gasquet belongs in their company it is worth mentioning that a week later he trounced Melzer in straight sets at Indian Wells.

Fortunately for France (although one might say fortune has nothing to do with it) its resources run deep. To the surprise of many, including no doubt Chardy himself, Forget decided to go with the would-be actor from Pau in the singles rather than Michael

Llodra, who was possibly still bearing the scars of that decisive final rubber defeat to Serbia's Viktor Troicki in last year's Davis Cup Final.

While Chardy would normally not be considered for a French Davis Cup team, he would be a fixture for many sides, and Forget must have seen something in his makeup or style that suggested he might spread his wings in the hangar. It certainly wasn't obvious to the rest of us: he hadn't won a singles match in nearly five months. As for the man himself, he still needed some convincing, and it took all of Forget's considerable experience as a player and a captain to do that.

"I told him just to look at it as a great opportunity," said Forget. "I said you've been playing tennis all your life to experience a moment like this—it's there. The guy's a great player, but if you play your best tennis you can give him a lot of trouble. Just think you're lucky, just enjoy the match and go for your shots, and if they go in, you could have a big surprise. And that's exactly what happened."

Chardy's aggressive approach certainly seemed to take Melzer—and Chardy himself—by surprise. "It's amazing for me, I played unbelievable," said Chardy, who had lost both his previous meetings to the Austrian in straight sets. "My tactics were to just play offensive, try to make a good serve, and then play with my forehand and go full on every shot."

Most of the six thousand spectators in the hangar must have expected Melzer to get back into it after a slow start, but when he was broken midway through the second set after losing the first, they knew he was in trouble. He had half a chance to salvage the set, when he broke the Frenchman at 5–3, but then kissed his hopes goodbye when, thanks to a double fault, he failed to consolidate an early break in the third.

Melzer later gave reasons for his 7–5 6–4 7–5 defeat but no excuses. "I think he played a great match," he remarked. "He was taking the game away from me, he was serving well and playing aggressively with his forehand, and I was never in charge of play out there. It's not my biggest strength if I have to react all the time and play from the back, but you have to give him credit for serving big and keeping his nerves together—of course I didn't play my best match, but he played a good one."

It was asking a lot of the thirty-four-year-old Stefan Koubek to redress the balance against Gilles Simon. Back in 2004 when he was beating the likes of Tim Henman and Greg Rusedski in Davis Cup play, he might have, but now the Frenchman made the 176-place discrepancy in their rankings count as he won 6–0 6–2 6–3 to give France a 2–0 lead.

Not that they would have admitted it, but France must have contemplated a two-day finish. Llodra and Julien Benneteau have developed a solid understanding in both Davis Cup and on tour, but Llodra didn't need reminding of just how good a doubles player Melzer was (the usual Melzer, that is). He and his regular partner, Nenad Zimonjic, had suffered at the hands of the Austrian (alongside Philipp Petzschner) in the final of the Rotterdam tournament the previous month; after all, Melzer and Petzschner were the reigning Wimbledon doubles champions.

There were other seemingly sound reasons for French optimism. Gilbert Schaller, the Austrian captain, had overlooked Julian Knowle, a former

US Open doubles champion, in favor of the much less experienced Oliver Marach, with whom Melzer had never even played. These captains know what they're doing, however, because the Melzer-Marach combination, a curious mixture of attack and defense, hit it off perfectly, winning 6–4 3–6 6–3 6–4.

Just as important as the result was the realisation for Austria that Melzer was back on song. If the pressure of knowing that he would probably have to play all three days had gotten to him, the physical demands clearly hadn't, judging by his display against Simon in the fourth rubber. The Frenchman, who had returned to something like his best in recent months, can grind opponents down, and Melzer had to stay with him for nearly four hours before suddenly finding his best form to sprint away with it, 7–6(7) 3–6 1–6 6–4 6–0.

So, by a slightly convoluted route, it had all come down to the fifth and final rubber, just as many always thought it would. And this was when France discovered Austria's Achilles heel, although not before their own legs almost gave way. The pressure of the occasion was all too much for Chardy at first, and he found himself a set and a break down against Martin Fischer, who plays almost exclusively on the Challenger circuit.

"My legs are like two pieces of wood," he told Forget. There are few captains in the game better at helping players in those moments than France's, and he got Chardy breathing properly—always the first requirement—and then bit by bit talked him back into the game. From there Chardy's strength did the rest against the tidy but lightweight game of his opponent, and with a 2–6 7–6(4) 6–3 6–3 victory, France was out of the hangar and on their way home. ●

Pictured above:
Hangar 3; France captain
Guy Forget; Austrian fans
Pictured opposite:
Oliver Marach (AUT) and
Jurgen Melzer (AUT);
Jeremy Chardy (FRA)

Serbia v India

While reigning champion Serbia proved it could win a Davis Cup World Group tie without its talisman, Novak Djokovic, it also showed, in this slightly fortuitous 4–1 victory over India, that it wouldn't be able to replicate last year's success without him. Perhaps Guy Forget, the France captain, was right after all when he suggested in Belgrade that while his own team had managed to get to the final without its No. 1, Jo-Wilfried Tsonga, he wasn't sure if Serbia could get there without Djokovic.

That said, neither Viktor Troicki, who assumed the mantle of No. 1 in absence of the soon-to-be world No. 2, nor Janko Tipsarevic were anywhere near their best as the team began the defense of its title. As it turned out, there were smiles all around in the Serbian camp because the team progressed to the quarterfinals, and Djokovic, who had opted instead to concentrate on the Masters events at Indian Wells and Miami, came away with two trophies in his luggage.

The people in charge of the sound system at Novi Sad's SPENS sports center had chosen to stoke up the atmosphere with an ancient battle song during changeovers, and it proved particularly apposite, because it wasn't long before the Serbs realized they had a fight on their hands. For a while it looked as if the home team was just carrying on where it left off

in December or, to be specific, where Troicki left off when he won that decisive final rubber against France's Michael Llodra.

The hero of the hour then sailed into a two-sets-to-love lead against Rohan Bopanna, a doubles specialist, and then all of sudden the serve-and-volley game of a player ranked 611 places beneath him disrupted Troicki's rhythm, and before he knew it the score was two sets all. Even the home crowd applauded some of Bopanna's play. Unfortunately for India, their birthday boy—he turned thirty-one that day—began to run out of wind. If nothing else, Troicki's serve seemed to hold up and his twenty-first ace of the match sealed a 6–3 6–3 5–7 3–6 6–3 win.

"I am not happy with the way I played and I really didn't expect such a tough match," a shaken Troicki said. "He's a doubles specialist and as such, he played a lot better than anyone might have expected him to. He kept breaking up my rhythm and I found it really difficult to get going. Hopefully, we can win the tie after Saturday's doubles to make Sunday's reverse singles dead rubbers."

And with that last comment he dangerously tempted fate. In the final against France, Tipsarevic came into the tie a trifle rusty, and it showed. Here, he came straight from Delray Beach, where he had made the final, losing narrowly to Juan Martin del Potro, and he looked ill adjusted. Sometimes you just can't win no matter what you do.

In both the first two sets against Somdev Devvarman he threw away three-game leads. In fact, he broke the Indian three times in the first set but still ended up losing it thanks to twenty-seven unforced errors. Then in the third set he wasted an opportunity to get back into the match at 5–3 up. Devvarman's

speed and groundstrokes eventually took him to a bizarre but entertaining 7–5 7–5 7–6(3) victory.

This encouraged India to think in terms of victory rather than damage limitation. "We definitely believe now we can win this tie, and we will go out there to give it our best shot," said an ecstatic Devvarman. "I feel for Janko because he probably didn't have enough time to adjust from Delray Beach, where it was a lot warmer and that much easier to serve."

Had India not been without their renowned doubles team of Mahesh Bhupathi and Leander Paes because of injury, Serbia might have been more seriously tested going into the final day. As it was, their replacements, Devvarman and Bopanna, put up a spirited fight against the fresher Serbian pair of Nenad Zimonjic and Ilija Bozoljac, and had Devvarman served better it might have gone to a fifth and final set. Unfortunately for the Indians, he dropped his serve five times throughout the course of the match.

Zimonjic, who is normally partnered by Djokovic, Troicki, or Tipsarevic, was joined by Bozoljac, with whom he hadn't played in Davis Cup for four years. The younger man took a while to find his feet, but eventually his serving and particularly his volleying improved, and Serbia was able to recover and take the lead after dropping the first set. India, at 4–1 up in the fourth, had a chance to take the tie into a fifth set but let it slip, and after saving three set points in a protracted tiebreak, the Serbian pair eventually won 4–6 6–3 6–4 7–6(10).

Troicki seemed better prepared mentally for a harder match against Devvarman and in the end didn't quite get it, which probably had something to do with the fact that the Indian No. 1 committed sixty-six unforced errors. Not even Rafael Nadal could overcome that sort of handicap. When a line call went Serbia's

way in the sixth game of the third set with Troicki two-sets-to-love up, Devvarman exploded in frustration and harangued the chair umpire for a good five minutes.

If he lost his concentration then, he soon regained it when he saved two break points in the ninth game to give India a slim chance of extending this tie. Any optimism in the Indian camp was soon extinguished, however, when Troicki made the most of three break points in the eleventh game, after which he served out for the match. His own statistics of eleven aces and forty winners proved too much for his opponent, and the 6–4 6–2 7–5 scoreline told its own story.

Released from any pressure, Tipsarevic showed what he can really do with a 6–0 6–1 win against Karan Rastogi in the dead rubber. "It was indeed a lot more difficult than the score suggests," Tipsarevic said of the overall victory, "and we will definitely need our best player, Novak Djokovic, back if we are to compete with Sweden in the next round on an even keel." ●

Pictured clockwise from top left:
Serbia captain Bogdan Obradovic
and Viktor Troicki (SRB);
Rohan Bopanna (IND);
Janko Tipsarevic (SRB)
and Viktor Troicki (SRB)

Sweden v Russia

No wonder Thomas Enqvist, the Sweden captain, had a smile wider than the nearby Viskan River after the first day's play against Russia, and it wasn't just because his team had taken a 2–0 lead. Sweden had been waiting, on and off, for about six years to see if Joachim Johansson, their former No. 1 player, could recapture his old splendor before injuries bedevilled his career, and in the picturesque town of Boras, in southern Sweden, he had given the clearest proof that he could do so by blowing away Russian No. 1 Teymuraz Gabashvili.

With Johansson backing up world No. 4, Robin Soderling, Enqvist and the rest of the team could dream of bringing the title back to Sweden for the first time in thirteen years. "He's going to be a strong player for us in the future," remarked Enqvist, who was still smiling as Sweden duly completed their victory on day two in the doubles.

A week later those dreams were in tatters, and Enqvist's smile had been wiped from his face as Johansson walked off the court after winning his first match at a Futures tournament in Switzerland and declared, "I'm done with this life."

This was the second time "Pim Pim" had retired from the game, and this time it looked final. It must have come as a huge disappointment to Swedish tennis fans, let alone Enqvist. Sweden has a great No. 1 in Soderling and a fine doubles pairing in Robert Lindstedt and Simon Aspelin; all they lacked was a solid No. 2.

"The motivation is not there. I'm quitting immediately," said the twenty-eight-year-old Johansson. "I know I can beat all the best in the world but it does not matter when I am no longer passionate about doing it. It has dawned on me here that I'm done with this life.

"For five years I have struggled against injury, and my goal has been to get in a position to be able to choose what I want to do. I am there now and I've made my decision."

All that, though, was for the future when Sweden set about taking advantage of a Russian team shorn of the services of their two best players, Mikhail Youzhny—who had just announced his retirement from Davis Cup—and Nikolay Davydenko.

Enqvist had surprised a few people with his selection of Johansson, who had played just a handful of tournaments in the previous three and a half years. He had also lost the last rubber he played, against Argentina in last year's opening World Group first-round tie. What is more, his opponent, Gabashvili, was ranked No. 76 in the world—673 places above Johansson.

Even a discrepancy like this can mean nothing in Davis Cup—not very often, mind you—and Johansson, who once climbed as high as No. 9 in the rankings, created a new variation on an old sporting adage: rankings are temporary, class is permanent. His bludgeoning serve (he famously once hit a world record fifty-one aces in a match he didn't win against Andre Agassi at the 2005 Australian Open) and his forehand both seemed to be working as well as ever as he battered Gabashvili to a 6–3 7–6(4) 6–4 defeat.

Here he hit a "mere" thirty-three aces, but it was his second serve that, not surprisingly, gave him the

most pleasure. "Since my first shoulder surgery I haven't really served that well on the second serve," he said, "but in the last month I've been trying to step it up and hit every second serve around the 200 kmph mark. I'm really happy with that and I only hit one double fault today."

That contrasted with eight from Gabashvili, who opened with a pair in his first game. He did his best to stay with Johansson in the second set, saving six break points to take the match to a tiebreak, but after that he was just overpowered by the big Swede.

It was much the same story in the first rubber. At the time of this tie not even Novak Djokovic had a better record than Soderling, who already had three titles under his belt and was 17–1 for the season. Andreev's ranking has slipped in recent times, and from an all-time high of No. 18 he was now No. 97 in the world. Like Gabashvili, he couldn't live with Soderling's power, and once broken in the first set he was easily beaten 6–3 6–3 6–1 as Sweden's No. 1 took his Davis Cup record in singles to 13–1. He is unbeaten in the event as a singles player since 2008.

Aspelin and Lindstedt are formidable doubles players in their own right, and although they go their separate ways on the tour they come together quite handily for Sweden. They had their work cut out for them against Dmitry Tursunov and Igor Kunitsyn, who are first and foremost singles players, but in a tense match eventually came up with the point Sweden needed.

Pictured clockwise from top left:
Igor Andreev (RUS);
Igor Kunitsyn (RUS);
Simon Aspelin (SWE) and
Robert Lindstedt (SWE)

The Russians saved two set points in the second set before leveling matters at one set all in a tiebreak. Then they had break points in each of the Swede's first two service games in the third set and were on the brink of going two-sets-to-one ahead in both the ninth and eleventh games after breaking the Swedes again, but each time they failed to serve out for the set.

Even in the tiebreak they had their chances. When Tursunov was serving at 5–4 a second serve was controversially called out and the double fault gave the Swedes the opportunity to claw their way back into it. The Russians had a set point on Aspelin's serve at 5–6 but again the Swedes hung in there. Tursunov took the disappointment to heart and wilted in the fourth set as Sweden ran out 6–4 6–7(6) 7–6(6) 6–2 winners.

"Davis Cup is nothing like the matches you play on tour—it's a privilege and tons and tons of fun," said Lindstedt. "Pressure, yes, but lots of fun."

Winning the two dead rubbers—Tursunov beat Aspelin 7–5 6–2 while Andreev beat Johansson 7–6(8) 6–4—put a false complexion on the scoreline, but it didn't fool Tursunov, who had been working hard to improve his confidence and ranking after injury. "I think there's quite a bit of readjusting to do for the team—for everyone really," he said. "Hopefully we'll be able to stay in the World Group." ●

Chile v USA

Jim Courier seems to have timed his arrival as captain of the United States Davis Cup team just perfectly. For the first time in years the Americans seem to be spoiled for choice—just like the best teams, as their No. 1, Andy Roddick, duly noted. They were without both Mardy Fish and Sam Querrey for a potentially tricky tie against Chile in Santiago, but it seemed to make little difference to the outcome.

Of course, the return of Roddick to Davis Cup competition after a year-long absence is expected to make a big difference to their chances, but as well as that it coincides happily with Fish finally realizing some of his potential and young players like John Isner and Querrey starting to mature.

"We will have the benefit of mixing and matching and we can have more match-ups," said Roddick. "That's what nations like France and Spain have been able to do because of their depth. We can protect ourselves and I'm excited. I've pretty much only been on four- or five-man teams but not six—we can pick each other up."

That was exactly what they had to do after Paul Capdeville had unexpectedly squared the tie on day one when he came from two sets down to beat Isner. Although the Bryan twins inevitably restored the Americans' advantage in the doubles, there was still a fair amount of pressure on Roddick to win the fourth rubber against Capdeville. After all, clay is his least favorite surface, but he felt fresher legs would win in the end and he was proved right.

"I don't see this weekend having any lows. A lot of the stuff out there you might think is a low is a learning

experience for my guys and myself," Courier said. "I liked the way all of our guys responded to adversity out there."

If it was a difficult tie for the United States it was no less so for the South Americans, who were still without their injured No. 1, Fernando Gonzalez. On top of that, their former Olympic champion, Nicolas Massu, was still trying to piece together his game after injury and had been losing regularly, even on the Challenger circuit.

Hans Gildemeister, the Chilean captain, however, was optimistic about his team's chances and forecast that "Nicolas is going to fight and not give any points away and I think the way he has played the last few days, he can do some damage to Andy."

As for Courier, he was, as they say, quietly confident. "I think I'm the right amount of nervous," said the successor to Patrick McEnroe. "I have that excited kind of nervous which is what I'd expect to have at the moment," he said at the draw. "I'm not sure what I'll exactly feel like tomorrow when we walk out there but it'll be a different experience. I've thought a lot about it."

Both captain and No. 1 must have been feeling a little apprehensive about their return to the competition, but at least Roddick hadn't been away for nearly twelve years like Courier. And while the crowd at

Pictured above:

Paul Capdeville (CHI)

Pictured below:

John Isner (USA)

Pictured opposite:

Andy Roddick (USA);

Nicolas Massu (CHI)

and Jorge Aguilar (CHI)

the Estadio Nacional was noisy, it wasn't unpleasantly so for the Americans.

"I felt pretty calm out there. In fact, you know I tend to feel calmer in away ties because you know you have to," Roddick said. "You want to go in there with a deaf ear toward anything going on and be a bit calmer."

Taking the first set quite comfortably helped. Massu needed to give the crowd something to get excited about and he did momentarily when he won the second set, but Roddick was always in charge. Massu double-faulted to lose serve in the third set and then lost his serve again in the fifth game of the fourth set from 40-love up. After that, Roddick winning 6–2 4–6 6–3 6–4 was a formality.

Playing in his home town as Chile's new No. 1, Capdeville did not want for motivation and he responded quite magnificently. Against the huge Isner serve (thirty-eight aces and twenty-four service winners) it was a case of waiting for his opportunity and taking it when it came. That can take some time; just ask Nicolas Mahut.

Eventually two consecutive tiebreaks went Capdeville's way instead of Isner's, and then finally in the ninth game of the final set, the American faltered. In fact, he had faltered in his previous service game but Capdeville failed to capitalize then on three break points. This time the Chilean did when, after another trio of break points, Isner netted a fairly simple overhead on the third and last. The pressure had finally gotten to the big American.

"The crowd was so important," said Capdeville. "Everybody was saying, 'c'mon Paul, you can do it,' and I thought in my mind 'yes, I can.'"

And he did, holding serve with great nerve to win 6–7(5) 6–7(2) 7–6(3) 7–6(5) 6–4 in four hours, twenty-one minutes. It was, of course, a crushing disappointment for poor Isner. "I'm really down, I let the team down," he said. "I didn't play well. He played better than me. I was winning and let him back in. I feel terrible, just terrible."

Isner could not have wished for a better doubles team than Bob and Mike Bryan to lift his depression, which the following day they duly did when they beat Massu and Jorge Aguilar 6–3 6–3 7–6(4) to record their eighteenth success in the competition. It put them

level with John McEnroe at third place in U.S. Davis Cup history for most doubles victories, behind John van Ryn with twenty-two wins and Stan Smith with twenty.

Just for a moment or two it appeared that Capdeville might stretch his heroic endeavors to a second point when he took the opening set off Roddick. A decisive final rubber was looming until the climax of the second set, when Roddick reeled off the first five points in a tiebreak to level it at one set all. When the Chilean dropped serve in the opening game of the third set it was like a blow to his solar plexus.

Suddenly the finishing line started to look a long way away for Capdeville, as another warm day began to take its toll on him mentally as much as physically. When he was broken again in the ninth game, the No. 2 players on both teams removed their hard hats, figuratively speaking. After winning 3–6 7–6(2) 6–3 6–3, Roddick commented: "My plan was to make him work hard. I knew I was fresher, I had better legs and that won me the match."

Victory for Isner in the dead rubber against Guillermo Rivera-Aranguiz by 6–3 6–7(4) 7–5 must have made him feel just a little bit better about himself. As for the U.S. team as a whole, it was looking forward to some home comforts after two years on the road. "There are a lot more home matches coming in our favor. It comes in waves, and that's a big part of Davis Cup in helping a nation win," said Courier. ●

Belgium v Spain

The great unanswerable of last year's competition was whether Spain would have lost to France had Rafael Nadal been playing. Perhaps more to the point, would Serbia still have celebrated its historic triumph? It seems almost ridiculous to suggest that one player could make the difference between victory and a 5–0 defeat, but the young man from Majorca is such a tour de force it's possible.

Spain didn't need him to beat Belgium. In fact, most of the time it doesn't need its No. 1 to beat anyone, and not many teams in Davis Cup history have been able to say that. Still, Albert Costa, the captain, must have been delighted to have him back—not to mention the country as a whole—and have him prove his form and fitness after that worrying injury in the quarterfinals of the Australian Open.

As it turned out, his opponent that day, fellow Spaniard David Ferrer, was the one to miss this tie, pulling out the day before the opening singles with an inflamed nerve in his shoulder. It was hardly good news for Belgium, because the No. 6 in the world was merely replaced by the No. 9, Fernando Verdasco. As far as his opponent, Xavier Malisse, was concerned it

was positively a disadvantage because the player he thought he would be facing when he arrived at the Spiroudome—someone he had beaten twice before, albeit several years ago—was not the "stranger" he took to the court three hours later.

Malisse had never played Verdasco before, so while you could say it was the same for both players, Verdasco knew whom he would be playing since the previous afternoon. Malisse didn't. But the thirty-year-old Belgian has been around long enough to know that these things can happen.

"I first heard about it when I arrived at the venue at about 11:30, and it does change your mind a little bit," he said. "All week you're thinking of playing one guy, and go to bed mentally preparing for that opponent, so to hear three hours before play that you're facing someone different does mess things about, but that's Davis Cup."

When Malisse held serve in the opening game and then had three break points on the Verdasco serve in the next, he could have been forgiven for thinking, "maybe this change of opponent isn't such a bad thing after all." Such positive thoughts didn't last long.

Pictured clockwise from bottom right:

Xavier Malisse (BEL);

Ruben Bemelmans (BEL);

Spanish fans

Pictured opposite:

Rafael Nadal (ESP)

Although Malisse held serve to love in three of his four service games in that first set, one break was enough to undo him. After that Verdasco just got better and better, and the eventual 6–4 6–3 6–1 scoreline was an indication of just how matters deteriorated for Malisse. Later in the tie Olivier Rochus, Malisse's teammate, expressed his regret that the court was "too slow." Try telling that to Malisse as those forehands from Verdasco whipped past him.

Belgium's only hope then was that Nadal was a little rusty after his five-week lay-off and that a Davis Cup rookie would spring a major surprise. They had as much chance of seeing Eddy Merckx win the Tour de France again. As Nadal remarked beforehand, "My body is fine. If I wasn't perfect, then I wouldn't be here."

One look at him in training confirmed that fact. Reginald Willems, the Belgian captain, had surprised some people by choosing the inexperienced but promising newcomer Ruben Bemelmans to face Nadal rather than the vastly experienced Olivier Rochus. But the outcome would probably have been the same either way. If nothing else it was a valuable experience for the twenty-three-year-old Bemelmans.

Playing in his first match since Melbourne, Nadal was obviously a little below par but happy enough with a 6–2 6–4 6–2 victory that extended his unbeaten run in Davis Cup singles matches to fifteen. In fact, he has only lost once and that was on his debut, when the experienced and dependable Jiri Novak of the Czech Republic outsmarted him. (We didn't know then, but it wouldn't be the last time he lost to a player by the name of Novak.)

Bemelmans, who had played Nadal once before at the Thailand Open a year earlier, won plenty of baseline rallies and impressed the world No. 1. "He has good potential and is a dangerous player," he said. "If he keeps improving and makes fewer mistakes, then I think he has a good chance of moving up the rankings."

Unless Belgium now won the doubles, the game was up for them. Before the first set was over, half the lights went out in the Spiroudome, forcing the umpire, Pascal Maria, to halt play temporarily. But it wasn't long before Feliciano Lopez and Verdasco put all of them out for the home team. Steve Darcis and Rochus had their moments, just not enough of them. The latter wasn't too downhearted about their 7–6(0) 6–4 6–3 defeat.

"I was out there with one of my best friends [Darcis]," said Rochus. "We have known each other since we were six or seven years old, so to be here on the Saturday—against the best team, and with nothing to lose—it was fantastic. For about ten minutes in the third set we were playing some amazing shots. We were having a lot of fun, but it's still tough to lose in straight sets."

There must have been an uncomfortable growing sense of déjà vu for Malisse and Rochus, who were a part of the Belgian team that lost 5–0 to Spain in Seville in 2003. The support the Spanish received in Charleroi was not far short of that in the Andalusian capital. As Nadal remarked, "It's been like playing at home and probably the best support we've had outside of Spain."

Fortunately for the real home team, a repeat whitewash was just avoided when, after Nadal had beaten Rochus 6–4 6–2 for his sixteenth consecutive Davis Cup singles victory, Darcis just managed to get the better of Lopez in the final dead rubber by the narrowest of margins: 6–7(4) 7–6(6) 7–6(3).

It was some consolation for Belgium, although their captain may have been stretching a point when he described it as "a fantastic final day." ●

Pictured above:
Feliciano Lopez (ESP);
Fernando Verdasco (ESP)
and Feliciano Lopez (ESP)

Pictured above
(from left to right):
Tomas Berdych (CZE);
Andrey Golubev (KAZ)
and his team

Czech Republic v Kazakhstan

Kazakhstan had given due warning of its capabilities with its unexpected whitewash of Switzerland in the play-offs the previous year. That was explained away for some by the absence of Roger Federer. When Radek Stepanek, the Czech Republic's aging warrior, pulled out on the eve of this tie due to illness, the alarm bells were surely ringing for the third-best Davis Cup team in the world, even if it was playing at home.

The Czechs have done incredibly well in recent years, reaching the semifinals in both 2009 and 2010. But they have relied heavily upon two men—Tomas Berdych and Stepanek—who in the more testing ties have usually been required to play three rubbers. They have complemented each other perfectly—not least in the doubles—and when one man was off his game the other invariably stepped up to the plate. Against the World Group debutants the team was suddenly exposed.

This is not to take anything away from Kazakhstan, which was even more impressive than it was when beating the Swiss. Jaroslav Navratil, the Czech Republic captain, was looking to Berdych, the world

No. 7, to win all three of his rubbers, but in the event it proved too big an ask. He had only once managed that feat, and that was against a modest Dutch team in 2006.

As last-minute replacements go, Lukas Dlouhy wasn't a bad one. But while he was a decent enough replacement for Stepanek in the doubles—he was, after all, a two-time grand slam doubles champion—he was never going to be a replacement for Stepanek in the singles. Those rather large boots would be filled by Jan Hajek.

Navratil handed the fourth place on the team to the junior world No. 1, Jiri Vesely. Although selected for the doubles, the seventeen-year-old Vesely, who had yet to play his first professional match on tour, would only figure in a dead rubber.

The Kazakhstan No. 1, Andrey Golubev, had made great strides in the game the previous year, and his Davis Cup record of 9–1 in singles must have been good for his confidence. Yet he looked a bit nervous in the opening rubber against Hajek, a player whom he had had a tough time beating in Rotterdam a year earlier.

The Czech team did not want for support in Ostrava. The local ice hockey team had even relocated one of its matches away from the Cez Arena to leave the field clear for them. And accompanying them every step of the way was a marching band in the making, replete with trumpet, drums, hand bells, tambourines, and maracas.

Not to be outdone, the Kazakhstan team had the president of their country, Nursultan Nazarbayev, with them all the way. In fact, at times he seemed to be advising them on tactics. In addition there were about two hundred Kazakhstan fans all dressed in turquoise T-shirts, plus one brave couple who spent the entire weekend in full traditional costume inside the well-heated arena.

Hajek appeared to be lifted initially as he took a two-sets-to-one lead and even had his chances in the fourth set to finish the match. It was only when Golubev took it into a fifth set that he took control, as the Czech wilted 7–6(4) 6–7(3) 1–6 7–6(4) 6–3.

There was now some pressure on Berdych to square the tie against Mikhail Kukushkin, who had had a run of first-round defeats coming into the tie. He gave Berdych some problems in the first set, and the Czech No. 1 had to come from 5–2 down in the tiebreak to win it. After that, he was firmly in control and ran away with the rubber to win in straight sets 7–6(5) 6–2 6–3 to help conserve his energy, which he would need, given the workload he could expect in this tie. He seemed in a good place mentally, too. "I'm so

happy to be back again and enjoying this Davis Cup atmosphere," he said. "You cannot get it anywhere on the tour, it is very special, unique."

Everything continued to go to plan for the Czechs on day two when, as expected, Berdych replaced young Vesely alongside Dlouhy in the doubles. Given how good a doubles player Dlouhy is, it seems amazing that the two men had only ever played together once before in Davis Cup, and that was in Berdych's first doubles rubber in 2006, which they won in straight sets against Morocco. However, they hadn't gelled subsequently, losing five out of five matches together on tour. Most of all, though, it was a reflection on how successful the Berdych-Stepanek axis had been, the two men winning seven of their eight doubles rubbers.

One would never have guessed any shortcomings, though, in the Czech pair's performance. They immediately broke Evgeny Korolev's serve and then Yuriy Schukin's to race into a 5–2 lead in the opening set. After that the Kazakhstan duo, who were playing together for the first time in Davis Cup, made them fight all the way to a 6–4 6–4 7–6(5) win.

Yegor Shaldunov, the Kazakhstan captain, had chosen to rest Golubev from the doubles, and his decision was about to be put to the test in the first of the reverse singles rubbers. Six sets of tennis in two days shouldn't have affected Berdych too badly, so maybe it was the mental pressure that got to him or maybe it was just Golubev. As far as Berdych was

Pictured above:
Kazakh fans;
Jan Hernych (CZE)
Pictured bottom left:
Andrey Golubev (KAZ)
Pictured opposite:
Mikhail Kukushkin (KAZ)

concerned, he thought his opponent played "a perfect match" in the first of the reverse singles on day three.

Whatever Golubev swung at in the first set seemed to go in. He hit twenty winners compared to Berdych's five. Even in the second set Berdych found himself on the ropes and had to come from a break down to level at one set all. Mentally, Golubev was totally focused while physically he was here, there, and everywhere, and after taking the third set he raced away with the fourth to win 7–5 5–7 6–4 6–2.

"I couldn't say one moment, one thing what he did wrong, he was just perfect," said Berdych. "I saw him play the match like this last year in Kuala Lumpur against Soderling—he beat him 6–2 6–2. That's just the way of tennis. He deserves respect for what he did today."

Suddenly, a team who had been thrashed 4–1 by Chinese Taipei just two years earlier was on the brink of another major upset. Kukushkin had sprung the biggest surprise of all in the play-off victory against Switzerland by beating Stanislas Wawrinka. Now he was the favorite, against Hajek, and he handled the responsibility admirably.

The rubber and the tie, though, were in the balance until the last knockings of the third set. Had Hajek won that—and he was serving for it at 8–7 in a tiebreak—the tie might have gone the Czech Republic's way. But just as in his opening match, he couldn't quite press home his advantage, and little Kukushkin, who is not afraid to go for his shots, reeled off three points on the trot to take the set. With that, Hajek visibly crumbled, allowing Kukushkin to complete a 6–4 6–7(4) 7–6(8) 6–0 win. Whereupon the Cinderella team of this Davis Cup season took itself back to its hotel to celebrate another famous victory with a dinner that started well past midnight. ●

Pictured clockwise from bottom left:
Mikhail Kukushkin (KAZ);
Yuriy Schukin (KAZ) and
Evgeny Korolev (KAZ);
Lukas Dlouhy (CZE) and
Tomas Berdych (CZE)

Croatia v Germany

If there is one name on a draw sheet that every one of the top players in the world likes to avoid, it's Ivo Karlovic. The giant Croatian was renowned for having one of the biggest serves in the game. During the course of his nation's first-round tie against Germany he earned a new sobriquet: the man with the biggest serve in history, at 251 kmph. Philipp Petzschner, a rookie who was in Zagreb ostensibly to play doubles, found himself on the receiving end.

A mismatch? Don't you believe it. Petzschner won 6-4 7-6(3) 7-6(5) to clinch the tie, and, in the words of Patrik Kuhnen, Germany's captain, "returned like he was playing against a junior, not a world record holder." Nor was it a fluke since it was the second time that weekend that the man from Bavaria had tamed him, having returned brilliantly against Karlovic in the doubles. German tennis, it would seem, had found a new hero at the ripe old age of twenty-seven.

"I knew that the winner would be the one who does his thing best: Karlovic's serve or me returning," said Petzschner. "Breaking the first game was a huge help—it was maybe my best game of the match."

Surprisingly, Petzschner, who is best known for winning the 2010 Wimbledon doubles title with Austria's Jurgen Melzer, believes his serve and his forehand from the baseline are his biggest weapons, rather than his power of return. Karlovic, along with a few thousand spectators at the Dom Sportova, might beg to differ. "I've never seen such returning. No one did that better against me than Petzschner," said a surprised Karlovic.

Florian Mayer was the player designated to play in the final rubber, but Kuhnen changed his mind after Mayer's tough five-setter against Marin Cilic in the opening rubber and Petzschner's performance in the doubles. "It was brave, it was wise, it was right," said Kuhnen.

Croatia, too, had planned to play someone else in the final rubber—Ivan Dodig—but after playing ten sets lasting over nine hours during the two previous days he was exhausted and replaced by Karlovic.

To be fair to the big man, he was still not back to his best after Achilles surgery that had kept him off the tour for nearly eight months and had seen his ranking plunge to No. 217. This was his seventh defeat in eight matches, but to his credit he made no excuses. "I did what I could," he said. "I fought the best I could, had some bad luck, had some chances, but it did not go my way. Petzschner was just too good."

For one reason or another this was not the Croatia of six years earlier, when they became the first unseeded nation to win Davis Cup. Ivan Ljubicic, their kingpin, had, to all intents, retired from the competition, as had, sadly, his doubles partner, Mario Ancic, from tennis altogether because of illness.

Coincidentally, it was during a Davis Cup tie against Germany in 2007 that Ancic first fell ill; he was later diagnosed with mononucleosis. Now, four years later, he was announcing his retirement from the game in the same hall where he played his first Davis Cup tie as a fifteen-year-old. It was an emotional occasion as he walked his final "victory lap." Afterward he said: "For me it was always something special playing for my country. I am proud that I had a chance of playing with 'Croatia' written on the back of my shirt."

Croatia's new No. 1, Marin Cilic, seemed to have suffered a reaction to being well beaten by Novak Djokovic in the previous year's historic quarterfinal between the two neighboring nations. His form didn't return until he reached the final of the Marseilles tournament immediately prior to this tie. And despite some health issues earlier in the week, he continued his revival with a gritty performance in the opening rubber, in which he came from behind to beat Mayer 4–6 6–0 4–6 6–3 6–1.

Cilic had lost to the German at Wimbledon in 2010 and at the Zagreb Open only the previous month, but, as he suggested beforehand, that had little bearing on the outcome of this match. Mayer's change of pace, however, makes him a difficult player to read, and again Cilic had problems with him in this respect, up until the third set, when an early break of serve handed the Croatian the initiative and he never let go.

"One of the reasons I lost was that set—should have won 6–1," said Mayer. "Then everything changed, he got the momentum, I was too defensive."

Karlovic had a 2–1 winning record against the German No. 1, Philipp Kohlschreiber, but Goran Prpic, the Croatian captain, opted to go with the in-form

player and he was not wrong. Dodig, who had won the indoor event in Zagreb the previous month, beating fellow countryman Ljubicic en route, had never played a live rubber before but showed few nerves as he took a two-sets-to-one lead.

Essentially, the match was decided by the outcome of the fourth-set tiebreak in which Kohlschreiber saved a match point at 5–6 down with a superb forehand and Dodig then surrendered with a double fault. Thereafter the German's greater experience prevailed in a 6–4 3–6 4–6 7–6(6) 6–4 victory, his fourth in Davis Cup five-setters.

world record did not affect the outcome of the rubber, as the Croatian doubles pair lost 6–3 3–6 5–7 6–3 6–4.

The Germans thought that a toilet break after that fourth set was the turning point. The Croatians, who took a toilet break at the same time, had been asked what was going on when both teams left the court. "I don't know what they've been doing there," said Karlovic. "I know what we did. They must have been doing something more than we did."

The home team had always won a tie between these two countries in the past, and in the reverse singles Cilic raised Croatia's hopes of maintaining that

Again, in the doubles, Croatia had the upper hand, with Karlovic and Dodig leading Christoper Kas and Petzschner by two sets to one. But it all changed in the fourth set after the Croatians suffered an early break of serve, thanks to some brilliant returning by Petzschner.

Coincidentally, this was also the set in which Karlovic thundered down his 251 kmph (155.96 mph) world-record serve, thereby breaking Andy Roddick's record of 249.4 kmph, which was also set in a Davis Cup tie, against Belarus in 2004. Needless to say, Petzschner got a racquet to it even if he didn't successfully return it.

Unlike Roddick, Karlovic did not take a bow, which may have been because he didn't know he had broken the record until his wife informed him afterward; she had read it on a website. Sadly for Karlovic, notching a

record when he took his second point of the tie by beating Kohlschreiber 6–2 6–3 7–6(6). Playing almost faultlessly in the opening two sets, he won 85 percent of his first serves and broke the German five times. Kohlschreiber, who had won three of their four previous meetings on hard courts, fought back in the third set but failed to capitalize on a 4–2 lead in the tiebreak. It was then Cilic's turn to stutter with a double fault at 6–5 before he eventually converted his third match point.

Historically, there was still one other factor standing in Croatia's way, which was that only once before had they come from 2–1 down to win. That was in their very first tie under their new flag in 1993 against Zimbabwe when Prpic, now their captain, won the decisive rubber—but then Wayne Black didn't return like Philipp Petzschner. ●

Pictured opposite
(from top to bottom):
Philipp Petzschner (GER)
and Christopher Kas (GER);
Florian Mayer (GER);
Philipp Kohlschreiber (GER)
Pictured above
(clockwise from main image):
Marin Cilic (CRO);
Germany captain Patrik Kuhnen;
Croatia captain Goran Prpic

Argentina v Romania

Argentina and Romania approached the season—and more relevantly their tie—in Buenos Aires sharing a bittersweet record. Or should that be sweet-bitter? Along with India, they have reached more Davis Cup finals than any other nation without once winning. Three times they have scaled the mountain only to fall from the summit just as they attempted to plant their flag.

More good news was that Monaco was back and Nalbandian was available despite injury, but the bad news was that the latter would have to have a hernia operation shortly after the culmination of this first-round clash. Also returning to the side, after a two-year absence, was Juan Ignacio Chela, ostensibly to play in the doubles in place of the injured Jose Acasuso.

It is widely believed that Argentina, if not Romania and India, has the ability to win Davis Cup but too often in the last couple of years it has found itself hamstrung by injuries to its leading men.

Indeed David Nalbandian has had to perform for much of the time in considerable pain due to a variety of abdominal problems, while Juan Martin del Potro, nominally their No. 1, barely played at all last year because of a wrist injury that threatened his very existence in the game. If that wasn't bad enough, the Argentine No. 3, Juan Monaco, missed most of the summer, also with a chronic wrist condition.

The good news for Argentina going into this tie was that del Potro, who had recently returned to competitive action, was improving in health and form with every match and had just won the title at Delray Beach. Furthermore, he had vowed that if Argentina overcame the Romanians he would return to Davis Cup for the next round.

The 5–0 thrashing Argentina received at the hands of France in last year's semifinals was not reflective of the country's standing in the game. Vazquez and his men were determined to prove this against Andrei Pavel's team, although as he conceded on the team's first return to the capital in two years, "playing at home is an advantage, but also a responsibility."

Romania had dealt decisively enough with Ecuador in the play-offs the previous September, winning 5–0, but they were now stepping up in class. Also, its fortunes are closely bound to those of its No. 1, Victor Hanescu, and he was no longer quite the player he was in 2009 when he rose to No. 26 in the world. Even so, the big man knows how to play on the red stuff and had had a couple of positive performances (if not necessarily positive results) going into the tie. He took Mardy Fish to five sets at the Australian Open after leading by two-sets-to-love and then lost a close three-setter to Stanislas Wawrinka on

Pictured above (from left to right):
Juan Monaco (ARG);
Eduardo Schwank (ARG) and
Juan Ignacio Chela (ARG)
Pictured opposite:
David Nalbandian (ARG);
Argentine fans

clay in the same city where he would now face Monaco in the second rubber. He wasn't best pleased with the draw, though.

"I would have preferred to play the first match, but in the end it is almost the same," he said. "I want to give Romania the point. I feel good right now, after a couple of weeks playing in South America to adapt to the conditions and the surface."

Having won his two previous meetings with Monaco on clay, Hanescu was obviously confident of giving the visitors an early lead and thereby adding pressure to Nalbandian's other concerns. By now, of course, Nalbandian is used to it. He was in similar poor health the same time last year when he decided at the last moment to try to help out his country in Sweden and made the difference between winning and losing.

"I feel good," he said unconvincingly. "I'm not 100 percent, but good enough. Davis Cup is completely different from the tour: the pressure, the people, the team. I enjoy very much playing in front of my own crowd."

"Enjoy" probably wasn't the word he would have used after his match with the relatively inexperienced Adrian Ungur. Although his win by 6–3 6–2 5–7 6–4 may have been fairly clear cut, it was anything but

comfortable. The troublesome hernia and an adductor tear to his left leg meant that he played most of the match in agony. Ungur threatened initially but only really delivered in the fourth set, when he converted the first of his eleven break points. Nalbandian staggered across the finishing line in tears, with the crowd giving him a standing ovation for his effort that had probably as much to do with emotion as actual pain.

"I can't walk a single step," he said afterward. "I thought I would be in better shape, but I have felt really bad since the first set. I've never felt that bad. I could finish the match because this is Davis Cup—it's impossible to leave the court. If it was a tournament from the tour, I would have retired in the second set. But here, I play for my country, with my people supporting me, and that is a great motivation."

The win was something of a milestone for this enigmatic individual, because it put him ahead of Jose-Luis Clerc in all-time Davis Cup victories for his country with thirty-two in singles and doubles play. He is now second only to Guillermo Vilas, but he has a long way to go before he can even dream of overhauling the great man. After this tie he needed just another twenty-six wins. One senses his body may have a say in the matter.

Pictured above:
The two doubles teams;
Argentina captain Tito Vazquez

Pictured clockwise from top right:

Victor Hanescu (ROU)
and Juan Monaco (ARG);

Parque Roca;

Adrian Ungur (ROU);

Horia Tecau (ROU)
and Victor Hanescu (ROU)

The pressure was now all Hanescu's, and he didn't make a particularly good start in a first-set tiebreak that was decided more by the nerves of both players than good play. After that it was all about extremes in the performances of both men. The powerful serve of the six-foot, six-inch Romanian came into play in the second set as Monaco's game lost its intensity, but the Argentine, who hadn't won a single rubber in two years, turned the match on its head in the third and fourth sets, winning 7–6 (5) 1–6 6–1 6–1. The only close call was who shed more tears afterward: Nalbandian or Monaco. As for Vazquez, he merely lost his voice.

Pavel remarked that Hanescu needed to "set his mind together" before the doubles the following day and made the mistake of tempting fate by suggesting that the Romanians were favorites to win the third rubber. In their position, one supposes, he could do nothing else but talk up his team's chances. In fairness, Hanescu and Horia Tecau had just won the doubles title in Acapulco in preparation for this tie.

But while Chela and Eduardo Schwank were playing together for the first time in Davis Cup, they had reached the semifinals at Wimbledon last year (when, by coincidence, it was Tecau and his regular partner, Robert Lindstedt, who halted their progress), so they were not completely without hope.

As it turned out, they won surprisingly easily, 6–2 7–6(8) 6–1, to wrap up the tie in double-quick time. Schwank went on to contribute a second point to the cause on the final day by beating Victor Crivoi 7–6(3) 6–2 in the fourth rubber before Ungur gained a consolation point for Romania with a 6–4 2–6 6–3 win against Monaco. The 4–1 win brought Argentina its eleventh victory in twelve home ties, the only blot on the record being the 2008 Davis Cup Final defeat to Spain in Mar del Plata. What it wouldn't give to avenge that. ●

Neale Fraser

Listening at home in Melbourne to radio commentary of the 1950 Davis Cup Challenge match at Forest Hills, the thirteen-year-old schoolboy's mind was made up the moment Frank Sedgman steered Australia to victory in the doubles. "Gee," he thought, "I want to be a tennis player and I want to play Davis Cup." Few men in the history of the game have gone on to encapsulate the spirit of the competition better than Neale Fraser.

Although an outstanding singles player, Fraser was first and foremost a team player, as his record in doubles would testify, and he didn't have to think twice about accepting an offer in 1970 to captain Australia's Davis Cup team.

Two years into the Open Era, honorary roles were not exactly keenly sought after, as Fraser would be the first to admit, but he made the position his own. During his twenty-four years as captain—the record Down Under for the longest time in charge—Australia won fifty-five out of seventy-five ties and hoisted aloft the Dwight F. Davis trophy on four occasions: in 1973, 1977, 1983 (without a single player inside the Top 30), and 1986.

Fraser's own playing career was adorned with grand slam title success—three in singles including Wimbledon, eleven in men's doubles, and five in mixed doubles—but it was the Davis Cup that provided him

with his greatest thrill—and his greatest challenge. First selected for the team in 1955, he had to wait three years to make his debut despite being one of the best players in the world at the time (and Spain thought they had strength in depth!).

That greatest thrill came in 1959 at the same West Side Tennis Club in New York that had him glued to a crackling radio as a boy. It was the stuff of dreams all right, because Fraser not only emulated Sedgman by contributing three points to the victory, but he also compensated for the "failure" of the incomparable Rod Laver, who had lost both his singles rubbers. It was indeed a proud day for Fraser as he beat Barry MacKay in the fifth and final rubber with his mother and father looking on.

As captain he set about putting together one of the greatest teams in Davis Cup history: the 1973 team. Having persuaded Laver and John Newcombe to return to the Davis Cup fold (both thought they were too old), he turned his attention to his personal favorite, Ken Rosewall.

"Rosewall was the greatest player over a period of time I ever saw," said Fraser. "He was in the final of Wimbledon when he was nineteen, and he was there again when he was thirty-nine. Amazingly, he told me he thought he might not be good enough to play for Australia. And I said, 'Ken, I would find it very hard not to pick you in any match we play.'"

Lo and behold he did, though. With Laver, then thirty-five, and Newcombe, twenty-nine, playing sublimely, Fraser was forced to tell Rosewall that he was not needed in the singles for the semifinal against Czechoslovakia and later for the final against the United States.

"It was one of the toughest things I've ever had to do," said Fraser. "I can still see the hotel room and the corridor around which I walked to his room to tell him he wouldn't be playing. His wife was with him at the time and she was a bit more proactive than Ken, which is understandable. I had to rehearse what I was going to say because I just wanted to do it and get out of there. He would have been No. 1 in any other team in the world."

Fraser, like many Australians, had taken up tennis partly to see the world but he realized he may have taken on more than he bargained for earlier that year when, prior to a tie against India in Madras, he was approached by the head of Interpol for Asia. He was warned that the Black September group had made death threats against his team.

"He said he wouldn't blame us if we decided to leave," said Fraser. "I asked the guys what they wanted to do, and the married ones like Mal Anderson wanted to go home while the younger guys said, 'That's good, we'll get to play.' In the end we stayed but it was a pretty hairy time."

In scenes right out of an Agatha Christie novel, the Australian team traveled to the practice courts each day in an armed convoy—they couldn't even go to the toilet without an armed guard. Meanwhile, the Interpol chief walked around in a white tennis hat with a revolver inside it, recalled Fraser. "I remember it was where I learned to play charades," he said surreally.

Just occasionally the job calls for a bit of pretense, and Fraser admitted to telling Pat Cash a white lie in his last Davis Cup final as captain, in 1986 against Sweden in Kooyong. In a must-win fourth rubber, the young Australian No. 1 returned to his chair after going two sets to love down against Mikael Pernfors to tell Fraser that he didn't think he could win.

"The only thing I could think of saying to him was, 'I might agree with you but I think he's tiring,'" said Fraser. "He said, 'Do you think so?' I said, 'Definitely.' He came back to win us the title in five sets." ●

LENDING THEIR SUPPORT

What separates Davis Cup from other tennis competitions is the fact that players are competing as a team. Nowhere is this more obvious than in courtside demonstrations of patriotism.

Quarterfinals 8–10 July

Spain defeated USA 3–1 AUSTIN, TEXAS—INDOOR HARD

Serbia defeated Sweden 4–1 HALMSTAD, SWEDEN—INDOOR HARD

Argentina defeated Kazakhstan 5–0 BUENOS AIRES, ARGENTINA—OUTDOOR CLAY

France defeated Germany 4–1 STUTTGART, GERMANY—OUTDOOR CLAY

Introduction

Every sports fan loves to witness a giant killing—it's what cup competition is all about. And when Kazakhstan lost to Argentina there were many disappointed followers of the game around the world, not just in the new Soviet Republic. The consolation was that the semifinal round would now be contested by arguably the four strongest teams in the world, which isn't always the case, and it was a mouth-watering prospect.

In three of the quarterfinal ties there was much flexing of muscles as France, Serbia and Spain demonstrated their strength in depth by resting top-ranked players or leaving them out altogether.

Once upon time Argentina was in that same luxurious position, but nowadays it has slightly fewer top-quality players to call upon, so it was wonderful news that the team was able to welcome back former world No. 4 Juan Martin del Potro after a two-year absence from the competition through injury.

Still, it would have been encouraging for captain Tito Vazquez that Argentina could manage the whitewash of Kazakhstan without the services of Davis Cup stalwart David Nalbandian. Similarly, France triumphed without troubling Jo-Wilfried Tsonga in the singles and Serbia only played Novak Djokovic in the doubles.

The new millennium's four-time champions, Spain, however, remained the team to beat. Its defeat of the USA in Texas with a rubber to spare spoke volumes of its character and determination, never mind its quality. ●

USA v Spain

Spain had won the Davis Cup final in 2008 without the services of the incomparable Rafael Nadal, so no one should have been too surprised by its victory over the United States in Texas without him—and yet most of us were. Maybe it was the Americans' home record against Spain (and most other countries, come to think of it), or maybe it was the fact that Andy Roddick had gotten his wish to tackle the Spaniards in his own backyard of Austin.

One thing was sure: not even the most blinkered Spanish fan could have expected Albert Costa's team—which, coincidentally, was exactly the same as the one that triumphed at Mar del Plata in 2008—to have had this quarterfinal all tied up by the fourth rubber. It's probably just as well for them they did. Roddick is pretty pumped up at the best of times, and the opportunity to clinch such a famous victory in front of his hometown fans would have placed an intolerable pressure on Feliciano Lopez in a fifth and final rubber, however well he may have been playing.

Even Costa had to chuckle after predicting, somewhat diplomatically, that Spain would record its first win on American soil 3–2, but 3–1? As is so often the case in tennis, the tie could have gone either way,

so close were all the matches. Jim Courier, the U.S. captain, said as much, but before anyone says, "well, he would," one should add that so, too, did Guy Forget, the France captain, the previous year after his team had, even more alarmingly, beaten Spain 5–0. So much of Davis Cup action is spent on a knife-edge, which is why it's so deliciously unpredictable.

When the draw was made, all that anyone could talk about was the impact the two leading protagonists, Roddick and Nadal, might have upon the proceedings. In the event, they were peripheral figures. No one uttered the name David Ferrer.

The man from Valencia is a top 10 player and has been for some time, but for some strange reason when

Of course, Spain's victory wasn't entirely due to Ferrer, although he symbolized Spain's determination not to succumb to the odds that were stacked against them: the speed of the court, the size and volume of the crowd in the Frank Erwin Center at the University of Texas, and, not least, a full-strength American team that included two top 10 singles players and arguably the best doubles team in the world.

By happy coincidence, Lopez came into the tie in the best form of his life. Although he had lost to Roddick seven times on the bounce, he had stopped the rot just a fortnight earlier in the third round at Wimbledon where, according to Courier, he had "served him off court" in straight sets, so it wasn't exactly a given that he would have rolled over against him had the tie gone to a fifth rubber denouement. His contribution was immense, as it needed to be.

The American team was in good spirits going into the tie, largely thanks to its host, Roddick. Since the week-long preparations covered Independence Day, and the Americans no longer hosted formal Davis Cup dinners, the Austin resident organized a barbecue on July 4 at his new home—or in what Bob Bryan described as his "two-acre castle grounds," replete with a golf driving range. The highlight of the event was a hot dog-eating contest—it being the day of the Coney Island hot dog-eating contest—which one of the practice partners won. "He wolfed down a ton of hot dogs— almost puked—but won $500," said Bryan. Presumably, the Spaniards, who according to Costa do their own "funny things," thought it safer to stick to the chorizo.

The opening rubber could not have been more evenly balanced, both in prospect and outcome. Mardy Fish, USA's new No. 1, and Lopez had each just reached the quarterfinals at Wimbledon—a career

Pictured clockwise from top left:
Andy Roddick (USA);
Spain captain Albert Costa;
Fernando Verdasco (ESP) and
Marcel Granollers (ESP);
David Ferrer (ESP)

the business end of a tournament is discussed, he rarely gets a mention. Those in the game know his true worth—including the Americans, one should hastily add. As Roddick remarked after being defeated by the world No. 6 in straight sets on the opening day, "I have too much respect for Ferrer to act like I'm stunned."

When it comes to competitiveness—an absolute refusal to admit a point has been lost—only Nadal comes close to him. His kind of running can break an opponent's heart.

"Ferrer is one of the toughest outs in tennis," said Courier. "I don't care where you're playing him, if you're playing him on the moon he's going to be a tough competitor and he's played Andy tough."

best for both. Fish had won their last three meetings, although it was 3–2 in head-to-heads. After the Spaniard's 4–6 6–3 3–6 7–6(2) 8–6 victory—his first five-setter in Davis Cup—he was asked what made the difference and replied simply: "After four and a half hours, to be honest, there's nothing that makes the difference. When you miss a few chances the omelette goes the other way. It was a very close match."

A couple of hours later Spain had the start they hadn't dared dream of when Ferrer beat Roddick 7–6(9) 7–5 6–3 in the second rubber. Costa could give himself a small pat on the back for that. At set point to Roddick in the opening set, a Ferrer shot was called out, but Costa was convinced the ball was in. "I saw that the ball was good," said the captain. "He [Ferrer] wasn't complaining, not saying nothing, so I yelled to him, 'David you have to challenge.'"

Ferrer did. He won the point and then leveled the score at 6–6 before going on to win the tiebreak against what he thought was a tired-looking Roddick. And some people say all captains do is hand out the towel! Before long Roddick was echoing Fish's sentiments about how tough it was to return to the locker room in such circumstances. "I can handle my own selfish losses but I felt I let my team down," he said. Asked if he thought he could pick himself up for the reverse singles, Roddick replied: "I hope I get that chance."

Courier could afford to be more philosophical. "I went through these matches in my head a lot and I'm not surprised we could lose these—I wouldn't have been surprised if we'd won them either," he said. "The atmosphere was everything we wanted it to be with the exception that we wanted an eruption at the end of one of the matches instead of silence."

It was certainly a strange-looking score line for day one, but as the local slogan says, "Keep Austin Weird." All Courier could do was bank upon his bankers—the Bryan twins—to bring about one of those crucial momentum shifts, and the new Wimbledon champions did not let him down, at least with regard to winning a point. That became a little more likely when the less-experienced Marcel Granollers replaced Lopez alongside Fernando Verdasco, although no one would have said that after the Spaniards won the first set.

"That's when you're happy that it's a three-out-of-five-sets match," said Bob Bryan. "You have a little more time to boogie-woogie. We knew we could settle down."

Such is the Bryans' record in this event—seventeen wins against two defeats—that few would have bet against the eventuality of another chest-bump celebration, which duly arrived upon completion of a 6–7(3) 6–4 6–4 6–4 win. With Bob coming from the baseline and Mike the service line, it took one's breath away just to see it. "We always break out the big chest-bump for Davis Cup," said Mike.

Pictured clockwise from top left:
Feliciano Lopez (ESP);
The Bryan brothers;
A USA cheerleader

Courier contented himself with the thought that the American team had "two better match-ups than on Friday" in the reverse singles, but history was heavily against them. Only once on thirty-eight occasions has an American team come from 0–2 down to win, and that was in a 1934 Inter-Zonal final against Australia in London when one Frank Shields, grandfather of Brooke Shields—the actress, model and, coincidentally, former wife of Andre Agassi—won the decisive final rubber.

The Americans could have done with Shields's distant relative against Ferrer, but in fairness to Fish, he put up a hell of a fight, just as he had done in his four previous Davis Cup singles matches, all of which went to five sets. Unfortunately for him the outcome for the third time was the same: defeat by 7–5 7–6(3) 5–7 7–6(5). "The hardest part was not being able to hand it off to Andy and see if we can win it," he said.

It was a particularly tough double loss for Fish, but at least his disappointment was shared equally throughout the team. "You lose a little piece of you when you lose matches like that when you want it so badly for the guys and for yourself," said Courier. "And I'm glad I feel that way, it's good to be emotionally invested in this. We definitely had our chances; we were up breaks in a lot of sets. This could very easily have been a 3–0 win for us. Credit the Spaniards, they're great competitors and they had a lot of chances that they let go also.

Courier had inherited, he said, "a very veteran team". For a man who as a player won the last of his four grand slams at the ridiculously young age of 22, it would be no surprise if the USA team now underwent a period of transition. As for Costa, it was a case of striking while the iron was hot with what he described as "an unbelievable generation of players" and he was in an avaricious mood. "We have to try to take advantage of this and win as much as we can," he said. ●

Sweden v Serbia

So much for "just a normal tennis team." The understatement of this Davis Cup year from Serbian captain Bogdan Obradovic fooled no one going into this quarterfinal, least of all his rival captain, Thomas Enqvist. The Swede probably knew for certain that his country had lost the tie against the reigning champion sometime earlier when Robin Soderling, the world No. 5, informed him that he would not be available for duty.

Couple that with the news that Novak Djokovic, the new world No. 1, would be available for Serbia despite the fact that he had only just come down from cloud nine after winning his first Wimbledon title and Enqvist could be forgiven for allowing his attention to wander to next season's competition, when life could become even more testing for Sweden, the seven-time winners. Not so Serbia, who must believe that victory in last year's final is only the start of a long and successful association with this competition.

"Davis Cup is always important," said Djokovic. "Me being here proves enough how I value this competition and how much I like playing for my country."

As it turned out, Serbia, to all intents, won this tie without its inspirational team leader. Between them, Janko Tipsarevic and Viktor Troicki garnered all the points in the 4–1 win in Halmstad. Mind you, it helps to know you have the best player in the world in reserve should you need him, so Sweden has no real need to reproach themselves about a missed opportunity. With or without Soderling, making home advantage count was always going to be a tall order for the Swedes. "He had to think about his health, and I respect that," said Enqvist of his missing main man, but Soderling's absence must have hurt.

The Serbs do seem to delight more than most in playing Davis Cup, which may be part of the secret of their success. Beforehand, Tipsarevic spoke of being excited at the prospect of spending a week with some of "my best life friends." We learned from one of his pre-match tweets that he could also be jumping out of a plane with them, too (hopefully with a parachute attached) should Serbia end up winning the competition for a second time. What is it about Serbia and close shaves?

He couldn't quite remember who came up with the idea of being a little riskier than last year with the celebrations should they triumph again (in last year's final, after beating France, it was fairly severe on-court haircuts all around), but he thanked them all the same for the extra motivation to realize one of his dreams. Obradovic's modesty obviously isn't catching. According to Tipsarevic, the goal was to win the competition "as many times as possible."

Djokovic was, in fact, selected to play in the second-singles rubber on the opening day and probably would have, despite his knee injury, had Soderling been around to open the scoring for the home team on a fast surface that he has relished in

Pictured above:
Nenad Zimonjic (SRB),
Novak Djokovic (SRB) and Viktor
Troicki (SRB) share a joke;
Ervin Eleskovic (SWE) is injured

Pictured above:
Simon Aspelin (SWE)
and Robert Lindstedt (SWE)
Pictured bottom right:
Viktor Troicki (SRB)

the past. The biggest loser, in more ways than one, was Ervin Eleskovic. Making his Davis Cup debut in his home country, the world No. 355 was looking forward to having "fun on the court" and to "see how far it takes me." The answer, sadly, was not very far—and it was far from fun.

As it happened, the Serbs chose to rest Djokovic, and Tipsarevic played instead. At 6–2 and 1–0 down in the second set, Eleskovic overextended his left knee on returning a serve out wide and was left writhing in agony with a torn anterior cruciate ligament. How ironic that beforehand Enqvist, in attempting to offset the disappointment of Soderling's loss, had remarked: "Nothing bad without something good."

It was a particularly cruel blow since it was injury that had stunted the Swede's development as a young player—a very promising young career as it happens. The Serbian-born Eleskovic had, in fact, once beaten Djokovic as a junior, although he couldn't remember doing so. Interestingly, Djokovic could. Eleskovic did remember beating Troicki, however. "I have beaten him and we trained together when I lived in Germany as a teenager," he said on the eve of the tie. "I thought he would quit; now he's a top player."

Not for the first time in his career, Eleskovic must have reflected again on the discrepant hands that fate can deal a young sportsman. Obviously it was not a victory that Tipsarevic could celebrate with any great

enthusiasm. Only too recently injury had forced him also to miss out on a treasured moment when he had had to retire in the final at Eastbourne, so he could sympathize to some degree with Eleskovic's plight.

"First of all I am very happy I brought the point to my country," he said, "but I am feeling really bad for Ervin and I couldn't imagine this day would finish this way. You really don't see too many retirements in Davis Cup, and this is just one of those days nobody wants to finish this way."

It hadn't started too well for Sweden either, although Michael Ryderstedt, assuming the role of No. 1, put on a performance against Troicki that can only spur him on to even greater things. Without wishing to detract from his effort against a player ranked all of 281 places higher, Troicki did appear to take his eye off the ball, perhaps literally as well as figuratively, at two-sets-to-love and a break up, just as had against India's Rohan Bopanna in the previous round.

"I was expecting it was going to be easy, and that's maybe why it wasn't easy," said the world No. 16. "I thought in my head that I had already won it, but it wasn't over."

Indeed it wasn't. It was a perfect illustration of how Davis Cup can motivate players to play above themselves, which is what Ryderstedt did, for the most part. He won the third set on a tiebreak and was

actually serving to take it to a fifth set, where anything could have happened, when tightness from the start of the match finally caught up with him. No wonder Troicki remarked, "I was lucky" after his 6–3 6–1 6–7(6) 7–5 win.

"I was trying to keep the points short," said Ryderstedt of his fourth-set tactics. "At that point I was getting way more tired than I should have. I was trying to stay aggressive but unfortunately I couldn't serve it out."

Sweden can boast more comebacks from 0–2 down than any other nation in the world, but a sixth one was never really on the cards here, even though halving the deficit in the doubles was. Sadly for them, Simon Aspelin had announced he would retire from the game after this tie (it was only recently that Enqvist had heard he had lost the services of Joachim Johansson), but at least the thirty-seven-year-old grand slam champion would be determined to go out on a high.

In an attempt to finish off the Swedes inside two days, Obradovic brought Djokovic into the equation alongside his doubles specialist Nenad Zimonjic, but as we all know, a singles pedigree doesn't count that much in doubles. Suffice to say that while Djokovic was No. 1 in the world in singles, he was only No. 236 in doubles. Lack of preparation by the Serbs didn't help matters, and the experience of Robert Lindstedt and Aspelin as a pairing was always likely to prove decisive.

An uncharacteristic overhead error from the Wimbledon champion cost Serbia the first break of the match and ultimately the opening set, but the Serbs briefly had their noses in front in a second-set tiebreak. However, with Aspelin, who won the 2007 US Open doubles title alongside Julian Knowle, returning superbly, Sweden won four points on the trot to take the set. Serbia had their chances in the third, and Lindstedt had to stave off four break points on his serve before his team came home 6–4 7–6(5) 7–5 winners.

It was only the fifth defeat that the remarkable Djokovic had suffered all year. Lindstedt, who unlike Djokovic had just come away from Wimbledon having lost a final (the men's doubles for the second year running), saw no significance in that whatsoever. "You can't compare singles to doubles," he said. "This is not the environment that he [Djokovic] is used to. If I played him in singles I would struggle to get games, but we are very happy to have played this well today and beat such a strong team as they are."

Going into the reverse singles the tennis shoe would now be on the other foot, since it would be Sweden's turn to pitch one of their doubles players into a "strange environment." Asked whether it had been decided which of them would have the "privilege," Aspelin replied that it had—"and I'm not happy about it," interjected Lindstedt, adding: "We'll see who wakes up with the less pain!"

As it happened, the Swedes were put out of their agony before Lindstedt could be thrown to these Serbian wolves. Getting his tactics spot on, a fully focused Tipsarevic never gave Ryderstedt a chance of adding further to his newfound reputation and ran away with the fourth rubber 6–2 7–5 6–3.

Serbia's attention immediately turned to their semifinal opponents, Argentina, or to be more specific, Juan Martin del Potro. Tipsarevic thought the outcome of the tie could depend on David Nalbandian's physical state upon arrival at the Belgrade Arena, but Obradovic was focusing on the lanky 2009 US Open champion from Tandil, who was coming back to his best form after a long absence from the game through injury.

"Everyone knows that del Potro doesn't play that much good on really fast surface," said the wily Serbian captain, going from understatement to overstatement. "He was not that good in Wimbledon and [on] some really fast surfaces. He likes hitting a high bounce so we will prepare something against him for sure." ●

Pictured above:

Juan Martin del Potro (ARG)

Pictured below:

Andrey Golubev (KAZ)

Argentina v Kazakhstan

The Davis Cup dark horse, Kazakhstan, had succeeded where Argentina had failed two years ago by defeating Czech Republic in Ostrava last March, so it should have gone into this tie not without hope.

In fact, when asked whether Argentina represented a similar threat to them as the Czechs, the Kazakhstan captain, Yegor Shaldunov, replied, "about the same." The reality was something quite different. Whether it was the Argentine capital's bitterly cold weather or the impregnable nature of the South Americans' Parque Roca venue-cum-fortress, Kazakhstan's players failed to repeat their earlier heroics in this competition and were thrashed 5–0.

Even Tito Vazquez, Argentina's captain, admitted that his team's passage to their seventh semifinal in the last ten years was "easier than expected"—

although it didn't stop him doing a headstand in celebration at the end of the tie. Goodness knows what acrobatics the sixty-two-year-old will perform if Argentina ever wins the cup.

What's more, the whitewash was achieved without their talisman for the best part of the last decade, David Nalbandian. Unable to play because of an ongoing adductor strain, Nalbandian was also unable to support his teammates on the opening day because the ash cloud from the Puyehue Volcano in Chile meant he was unable to fly to Buenos Aires. No matter. By the end of the first day's play, Argentina had whipped up a storm of its own, and on day two, Nalbandian, having driven from his home in Unquillo, arrived in time to support his replacement, Eduardo Schwank, in the decisive doubles rubber.

Buenos Aires may have been at a virtual standstill because of the upcoming government elections, but the country's players certainly weren't. Not since Great Britain—minus the services of Andy Murray—visited the Argentine capital three years ago had a visiting team won as few games on the opening day as Kazakhstan. On that previous occasion Jamie Baker and Alex Bogdanovic won just twelve games between them, but the difference this time, as Vazquez pointed out, was that the Kazakhstan players were ranked in the top 50 and 70 as opposed to the top 200 in the case of the Britons.

Nalbandian's temporary absence was more than offset by the return of Argentina's No. 1 player, Juan Martin del Potro, which Vazquez described as "a great happiness." The last time the former world No. 4 had represented his country was in that defeat to Czech Republic, when he contributed both his team's points. That was a couple of months before he won the US Open, beating Rafael Nadal and Roger Federer en route to his first grand slam title. It was shortly thereafter that he suffered a serious wrist injury that questioned the then-twenty-year-old's very future in the game.

However, the Tower of Tandil eventually righted himself, returning to the tour proper in January 2011, and bit by bit regained much of his form and fitness. He had gone out of the Australian Open in the second round but within a month had made the semifinals in San Jose and Memphis before claiming the title in Delray Beach. Another title followed in Estoril a couple of months later, which pushed his ranking up to No. 32. Grand slams, like miracles, would obviously take a little longer.

He admitted to being a trifle nervous about his return to Davis Cup. Try telling that to Mikhail Kukushkin. The star of the 5–0 whitewash of Switzerland in 2010 was blown away by del Potro in the second rubber, losing 6–2 6–1 6–2, a scoreline that the Argentine generously described as "a bit of a lie." Kukushkin, who was facing the Argentine for the first time, noted that del Potro had "no weaknesses," adding with obvious reference to his opponent's six-foot, six inch frame, "he even moves very well."

As for del Potro he declared himself, "Very happy. I had many different sensations playing here, in front of the crowd, and also in front of my family and friends. They have supported me all the time, on and out of the court. It's very nice for everyone. I think the circle is close now.

"I tried to be in good shape as soon as I can. It's a long road but I'm still trying to improve my game. I'm having a good season so far and there still remains the hard court season, which I like a lot. I think it could be a nice year if I finish top 10."

Lack of form and more specifically lack of success on clay by the Kazakhstan players may have been the biggest factor in their demise. Andrey Golubev, the Kazakhstan No. 1, had lost ten of his previous eleven matches going into the tie—which he attributed to poor health—while only Kukushkin had registered any victories on clay during the year. When told that that was the case he seemed quite taken aback. "Is it really this?" he asked.

Vazquez's only selection poser was which of the two Juans to choose as his No. 2: Juan Monaco or the veteran Juan Ignacio Chela. Chela, who was almost thirty-two, had been enjoying something of an Indian summer to his career, having reached the quarterfinals at Roland Garros a month earlier.

Vazquez had nicknamed him "Torino" after a vintage car that was once produced in Argentina. A couple of days before the tie, YPF, the Argentine oil company and the team's main sponsor, brought a real Torino race car that is being driven by the former Formula One driver Norberto Fontana to the Parque Roca for a fun photo shoot involving player, driver, and car. As for the "race" in hand, Vazquez opted to go for the current rather than the vintage model.

It turned out to be an inspired choice, because Monaco produced what he believed was the finest Davis Cup performance of his career in beating

Pictured below:
Argentina captain Tito Vazquez performs a headstand;
Mikhail Kukushkin (KAZ)

Pictured above:

Juan Monaco (ARG)

Pictured bottom right:

Eduardo Schwank (ARG) and

Juan Ignacio Chela (ARG)

Watching Chela and Schwank storm to a 6–3 6–2 7–5 victory against Evgeny Korolev and Yuriy Schukin may have helped erase Coria's disappointment of just having seen his favorite football team, River Plate, relegated for the first time in its history. "Watching Argentina in Davis Cup from behind the bench makes me want to step into the court again," said the twenty-nine-year-old Coria, whose career, sadly, finished long before it should have after he developed problems with his serve.

In some ways Chela's resurgence has been the answer to Vazquez's prayers. Once Horacio Zeballos and Schwank stopped playing together he needed a new partner for the latter. The combination of experience and youth worked well. "I love this sport, it's my passion," said Chela. "I'm really happy to be in the team again and I think we played a great match today. Even though the final set was a bit tough, we won in straight sets and gave Argentina the point."

To their credit, the Kazakstan fans continued blowing their own trumpets—in a musical way, of course—and thumping their drums throughout the final day's further reverses, accompanied by the Argentine fans. Korolev, winning his team's first set of the tie in the first of the dead rubbers, lost 2–6 6–2 6–0 to Chela, and then Kukushkin lost 6–4 6–1 to Monaco. Nevertheless, there was plenty of pride for the Kazakhs in the way their team had performed on its debut in the World Group and in the last ten months in general.

As for Argentina, it had more reason to look forward than back, and Vazquez was already contemplating what kind of surface Serbia, their semifinal opponents, would have waiting for them in Belgrade, which was bound to be something fast. "I would do the same thing," he said. ●

Golubev 6–3 6–0 6–4 in the opening rubber. In truth it was a contest for only the first five games. Once Golubev had been broken there was no doubt about the outcome. Nine games in a row later put Monaco in a commanding position, but it has to be said he was somewhat aided by his opponent's seventy-two unforced errors.

"It was a perfect day for me," said Monaco. "All the things I tried worked perfectly well. I played unbelievable every break point, all the time. I think it could have been my best Davis Cup match so far."

Not so for Golubev, who blamed the one-sided defeat on being too aggressive on a humid court rather than waiting for Monaco to make mistakes. Vazquez had warned beforehand that the cold conditions meant the ball wouldn't fly like it normally does. "I played bad and he played good," Golubev said succinctly.

The tie had begun a day sooner than the other quarterfinals in order that it be finished before the elections that Sunday. In the event, the tie was as good as over by Friday. Watching from the sidelines along with Nalbandian were former Argentine Davis Cup players Agustin Calleri and Guillermo Coria.

Germany v France

Only three teams in the world could afford to do what France did in Stuttgart and survive to tell the tale, and oddly enough they all did it, either by choice or necessity. They each contested the opening-day singles matches of a quarterfinal tie away from home without their best player. Furthermore, all three closed out their ties without recourse to a fifth and final rubber.

Serbia, Spain, and France stand head and shoulder above the rest of the world in Davis Cup, which doesn't mean they are invincible against the other countries of the world. But it does mean that when opportunities present themselves to their opponents, like a two-sets-to-love and 5–4 lead, they have to be grasped with both hands.

Germany had such an opportunity in the opening rubber at the Weissenhof Club, the home of the Mercedes Cup, when Florian Mayer took on Richard Gasquet, but he let it slip—or rather, his cramping thighs did—and after that there could be only one outcome to the tie.

Unlike Serbia and Spain, France's "best" player is a little less obvious. In fact, at the time of the quarterfinals, according to the ATP rankings, Jo-Wilfried Tsonga was only France's third-best player, but few would argue about his standing in French tennis. After his momentous victory against Roger Federer in the quarterfinals of Wimbledon, Guy Forget, the France captain, chose to rest him from the opening day's singles rubbers.

Because of his selfless commitment to the French cause and his love of Davis Cup, Tsonga is one of those players who accepts such a decision without complaint. He is also one of those rare individuals who manage to keep sport in perspective. Where some players fear the pressure that comes with representing one's country, he seems to embrace it.

"I just feel great in this competition," he said. "I'm playing for my country, but I think it's more than playing for my country. I'm playing with friends, people I like. It's country against country but it's not a worry, it's just a game. It's just so nice."

When a country takes on France, that country knows it is taking on a team in every sense of the word. It's apparent from the moment a tie begins and the French link arms while the Marseillaise is played.

There's a unity about them that isn't obvious in many teams. Gilles Simon, ranked 18 in the world, was given the role of cheerleader this time and just got on with it. Last time it was Gasquet who was omitted from the lineup, but as he said quite eloquently for a man who is unnecessarily embarrassed about his English, "We let the key to someone else, but we trust everyone."

It was at the Schleyer Halle in Stuttgart that Boris Becker put on his one-man virtuoso performance to win the 1989 Davis Cup final for West Germany against Sweden, beating Stefan Edberg and Mats Wilander in the singles as well as partnering Eric Jelen to victory in the doubles. Unfortunately for Germany, another bit of history was more relevant to this tie: their loss of fifteen consecutive live rubbers against France going back to 1953, when Gottfried von Cramm managed to beat Paul Remy.

Somewhat surprisingly, Becker, who was in the audience along with his fellow legend Michael Stich, never played a singles match against France (he lost the doubles in straight sets against them when Forget was on the opposite side of the net), while Stich never played France at all. Lucky devil, Patrik Kuhnen must often think. He's faced them three times alone since he became Germany's captain in 2002, but he must have gotten a whiff of an opportunity when Forget decided to give Tsonga a little longer to recuperate from his Wimbledon exertions.

Pictured above (from left to right):
Philipp Kohlschreiber (GER);
Philipp Petzschner (GER)
Pictured opposite:
France captain Guy Forget,
Jo-Wilfried Tsonga (FRA)
and Gael Monfils (FRA);
Richard Gasquet (FRA)

"We know the history," commented Philipp Kohlschreiber. "We are going to do our best to change the future—that's the only chance we have, as we cannot change the past."

It had been a good year so far for German tennis, even if it was the German women who had been hogging the headlines—and the picture space. Andrea Petkovic, Julia Goerges, and Sabine Lisicki are as photogenic as they are charismatic. But Germany's men had also been quietly making progress in the game. Their No. 1, Florian Mayer, had been enjoying an excellent year, particularly on clay, and at the age of twenty-seven had finally made the top 20.

As a result, the German team was quietly confident about the opening rubber, once it was announced that Gasquet would replace Tsonga, if not the tie itself. Gasquet has an indifferent record in Davis Cup singles—which was five wins, five defeats at the time—and when he went two-sets-to-love down and Mayer was serving for the match in the third, Baron von Cramm must have been readying himself to move over.

Only once in his career had Gasquet come back from two sets down to win, but nerves, unfortunately for Mayer, don't usually take account of the other man's weaknesses. Suddenly the German started cramping in both thighs. In each of the first two sets,

after dropping serve, he had reeled off four games on the trot to take command, but when he needed to serve out one game to win it proved beyond him.

Mayer had feared that each man's best shot—the backhand—might cancel one another out. As it turned out his mix of serve-and-volley, slice, drop shots, and angles gave Gasquet no rhythm. Now the Frenchman was able to dictate matters with a steady baseline game, and he turned it around to win 4–6 4–6 7–5 6–3 6–3 in three hours and forty-two minutes to record only his fifth five-set victory in sixteen attempts.

"I felt it at 4–4 for the first time," Mayer said. "I've never had cramps in my life, and I'd drunk enough, both before and after the match, so it must have been the tension. I could barely move in the fourth and fifth sets. It's a very bitter defeat because I was the better player for three sets but couldn't finish it."

Before that third set turned around, Kohlschreiber must have been reasonably relaxed about playing Gael Monfils. Now there was a different pressure upon him. He had beaten the athletic young Frenchman just a month earlier in straight sets on grass at Halle, but as he rightly said, "I think we can't count that."

This was like the usual summer in reverse, moving from grass to clay, and the outdoor surface afforded Germany no real advantage over its opponents. Monfils and Kohlschreiber played out

Pictured above (from left to right):
Jo-Wilfried Tsonga (FRA)
and Michael Llodra (FRA);
Gael Monfils (FRA)
Pictured bottom right:
French fans

a typical clay court match from the back of the court in which the Frenchman proved a little strong. He could always rely on his big serve to get him out of trouble, which it did when he had four break points against him at 4–4 in the first set. He went on to win 7–6(3) 7–6(5) 6–4.

"I think I was a bit more aggressive," Monfils said, "and that was the key. He was serving well, and also returning well, so I had to make it a physical match, a little more aggressive in the big points, and not miss."

At 2–0 down, the doubles rubber merely offered Germany the opportunity to delay the inevitable. Neither pair play that much together, but the Germans were hoping that Philipp Petzschner and Christopher Kas could rekindle some of the magic that had helped them pull off a famous victory against Croatia in Zagreb in the previous round.

Their best chance against Michael Llodra and Tsonga came and went at the end of the first set when a pair of double faults from Llodra enabled them to break for a 6–5 lead, only to be broken themselves to love when Kas made three simple errors at the net. Twice the Germans led again with mini-breaks in the tiebreak only to be undone by volleying errors at the net.

The Germans rallied momentarily in the third set when they had two break points at 4–3 on Llodra's serve, but their return of serve betrayed them, and they ended up losing the rubber and the tie 7–6(4) 6–4 6–4, making it eighteen consecutive live rubbers they had lost against the French.

The dead rubbers were shared one apiece, but France would happily have traded both for two wins from the USA against Spain in Texas. An eight-hour time difference between the two countries meant that celebrations in Germany were understandably somewhat muted. An American victory in Austin would have meant a home tie for France in the semifinals—Roland Garros had already been earmarked for the occasion. It was not to be, and instead they got the bullring in Cordoba, where only the very best of both teams would do. ●

Niki Pilic

It is ironic that the man who was central to the Wimbledon boycott of 1973, as a result of his ban for refusing to play for his country, should become one of Davis Cup's most iconic figures and greatest supporters.

This year marked half a century since Niki Pilic first competed in a Davis Cup tie. Fifty years on, and he has won the trophy with three different countries—a record that will surely never be broken. In all, he won it five times: three times as captain of West Germany, once as captain of his native Croatia—which he had led from out of the Europe/Africa Zone—and once as an advisor to Serbia.

Back in 1973 playing Davis Cup was compulsory, so when Pilic refused to do so for Yugoslavia in a Europe quarterfinal tie against New Zealand in Zagreb, he was banned for one month by the International Lawn Tennis Federation following a complaint from the Yugoslav federation (of which his uncle was the president!). The ban encompassed Wimbledon, and in protest the Association of Tennis Professionals boycotted the Championships, which led to many of the game's leading players missing the event.

"I told them that if I reached the final of the Masters doubles in Canada, which I did, I would not be

able to play in Zagreb because I felt I had a responsibility to my doubles partner, Allan Stone," he said. "Yugoslavia lost—surprisingly—and they needed a scapegoat. I was that scapegoat."

However, Pilic was back playing Davis Cup the following year and still believes that players should play in the competition if at all possible. "You can be a champion but if you do something different for the nation then you will be a Robin Hood, which means everybody will celebrate."

Pilic had to wait until 1988 before he finally won the Davis Cup, as a captain. But the wait was worth it. Against all the odds, he led West Germany to a 4–1 victory in Gothenburg against a Swedish team containing Mats Wilander, Stefan Edberg, and Anders Jarryd. The victory was special to him, not least because Germany had only one world-class player in its team at the time: Boris Becker.

They won the Davis Cup again the following year when Pilic had to deal with the problem of divided loyalties in the semifinals as they beat Yugoslavia 5–0. Goran Ivanisevic was playing for the opposition and living in Pilic's house at the time. A similar problem cropped up in 2010 when he was advising the Serbian team and they drew Croatia in the quarterfinals. The tie was held in Split, where Pilic was born, but he decided not to attend. "There was a nationalistic feeling there and I didn't want to be involved in that," he said.

Not that he hadn't had to deal with bad feelings before—even inside his own camp. Becker and Michael Stich famously didn't get along, and although they never won the Davis Cup in harness—Stich spearheaded the side in 1993 when Pilic won it for a third time—they did come together memorably for a short period. Pilic recalls the side that defeated the Netherlands 4–1 in a quarterfinal in 1995 as the strongest team he ever worked with.

"Both Boris and Stich were Wimbledon champions but they could also play unbelievable doubles—they won the Olympic title the year before without talking to each other," said Pilic. "Against the Dutch, they beat the No. 1 pairing in the world in Paul Haarhuis and Jacco Eltingh. They only ever lost one rubber, against the Russians in Moscow."

Pilic lost just one tie at home in eleven years with Germany. He also had an extraordinarily good record against the United States, which he beat five times out of six as a captain and advisor. When he became captain of Croatia, he oversaw victory against a very strong American team consisting of Andy Roddick, Andre Agassi, and the Bryan brothers in a World Group first-round tie in Los Angeles. Ivan Ljubicic and Mario Ancic were not exactly household names at the time—"they didn't even know who we were at our hotel," he said.

For Pilic, the captain's role is about having respect for the players—"without it, forget it." It's about convincing someone like Becker that "McEnroe doesn't have a fifth gear any more" or that he should stay back on his second serve against Agassi and then be proved correct. Or persuading a jet-lagged Novak Djokovic that he must play in the doubles (against Czech Republic) to get a feel of the court and the ball before the reverse singles. But also, he said, it's about getting the little things right.

"It's about telling the kitchen that you want the spaghetti at 1 p.m. not 1:15 p.m.," he said. "When you add all these small things together, the whole team becomes easier to handle and all that the players need to do is take a racket and go on court. But it takes a lot of energy because you then play every point with them. It drains you. But it has given me enormous satisfaction and I am happy that I did the best I could do in my life." ●

A WORD IN YOUR EAR

It might be that they are talking tactics, or maybe they are simply trying to make their
teammate's laugh, but players always find time for a private chat while the draw takes place.

Semifinals 16–18 September

Spain defeated France 4–1 CORDOBA, SPAIN—OUTDOOR CLAY

Argentina defeated Serbia 3–2 BELGRADE, SERBIA—INDOOR HARD

Introduction

The semifinal round of the Davis Cup by BNP Paribas was all about the impact that Novak Djokovic and Rafael Nadal would have upon their respective ties so soon after their delayed US Open final. Both men arrived at their destinations late, largely unprepared, and, in the case of Djokovic, hurting. The other crucial difference was that Djokovic had arrived a further two days later and less than twenty-four hours before the start of play because of media commitments in New York.

Had this been anything other than a Davis Cup semifinal, both men would almost certainly have withdrawn. But these moments come so rarely in a player's career—although not so in Nadal's and probably not in Djokovic's—that neither was prepared to pass up on the opportunity of winning one of sport's most prestigious team competitions. Nadal was aiming at a fourth Davis Cup title, while Djokovic had his heart set on a second successive one.

Neither Spain nor Serbia could afford to be without them. Spain had defeated the United States in Texas in the quarterfinal round without Nadal, but with all due respect to the Americans, Albert Costa, the Spanish captain, could ill afford to be without him against France. Djokovic hadn't played in a singles rubber all season, but Bogdan Obradovic, the Serbian captain, desperately needed him to do so against Argentina.

In the event, it was too much to ask of Djokovic, who broke down in the fourth rubber against Juan Martin del Potro. In fairness, Nadal did not have to cope with that kind of firepower against France, although he did have to contend with Jo-Wilfried Tsonga, who, as it turned out, was sadly out of sorts in their rubber. Nor was Nadal in any obvious pain.

Even so, it was a superhuman effort by Nadal to win both his matches and to do so without dropping a set. Some had feared there would be a hangover from his defeat to Djokovic in New York. They should have known better. It probably helped that the tie was on clay. The world No. 2 is happiest when playing in the red dirt. There probably isn't a player in the world who can make the transition from hard court to clay court so seamlessly. One is tempted to say that it is reminiscent of Bjorn Borg's capacity to switch from clay to grass in the blink of an eye, but then Nadal has managed that, too. ●

Pictured clockwise from top right:
Rafael Nadal (ESP);
Richard Gasquet (FRA);
Feliciano Lopez (ESP) and
Fernando Verdasco (ESP);
Spanish fans

Spain v France

By the time Fernando Verdasco had rubbed salt in the wound by winning the dead rubber—also in straight sets—France's whitewash of Spain in Clermont-Ferrand fourteen months earlier must have felt so long ago to Guy Forget and his team that it might just as well have been part of the Four Musketeers' glorious history.

Tennis players and Davis Cup captains are always keen to shift the burden of favoritism to the opposition prior to a match, but you knew the French captain meant it when he said before a ball had been struck in this one: "Spain is the best team in the world—by far."

Forget knew that maintaining France's excellent record in World Group semifinals (seven wins out of ten) was going to be tough in the converted bullring of Cordoba's Plaza de Toros de los Califas and that their chance of prevailing wasn't much better than that of the poor bulls who more often dignify this arena. But even he must have been a little surprised how easily

his team was put to the sword. In fact, the tie was one-sided throughout, since even France's single point, in the doubles, was comfortably won. It was in stark contrast to Clermont-Ferrand, where, as he had generously pointed out, every rubber could easily have gone either way.

During the previous year's final against Serbia, Forget had had a little dig at the opposition when he doubted whether they could have reached the final without Novak Djokovic as they had done themselves without their No. 1, Jo-Wilfried Tsonga. Now, as luck would have it, they would have to try to do so again without their No. 1, who this time was Gael Monfils. They had the Spanish to thank for that, since it was in a tough five-setter against their former world No. 1, Juan Carlos Ferrero, at the US Open that Monfils had aggravated his knee injury.

Forget tried a little kidology beforehand when he suggested that France was "just as strong" without the athletic Monfils. They clearly were not, and he conceded as much after the tie when he described him as "our best chance on clay." The truth was that Spain was so good in the singles that Monfils would have made little or no difference to the outcome.

Probably France's best hope—like Argentina's in the other semifinal—was that the US Open finalist of just four days previous would arrive at the tie unfit to give a good account of himself. But it was as forlorn as another theory mooted that Rafael Nadal might be vulnerable due to lack of clay-court practice. (There was more chance of a duck sinking after a week out of the water than Nadal floundering on clay.)

Forget controversially chose to omit Tsonga from his singles lineup on day one, but even the player himself conceded that it was a "logical" decision. He hadn't gone beyond the third round at any of the season's clay court events, so it was only proper that Gilles Simon, who had excelled on the red stuff, winning the Hamburg tournament, assumed the role of No. 1 while Richard Gasquet was handed the dubious pleasure of starting against Nadal.

The French, who had spent the best part of the week practicing in high temperatures, were relieved to see that it had dropped a few degrees on the opening day. However, the heat, figuratively speaking, remained firmly on them. Gasquet was competitive for no more than three-quarters of an hour, during which time the

Pictured clockwise from top left:
David Ferrer (ESP),
Rafael Nadal (ESP) and
Spain captain Albert Costa;
Plaza de Toros de los Califas;
Gilles Simon (FRA)

loyal followers of Les Bleus kept fingers and toes crossed that he would change the habit of a lifetime by beating Nadal, something he hadn't managed since they first met in a Challenger event at St. Jean de Luz eight years and ten meetings earlier when the then seventeen-year-old Mallorcan retired.

Losing a tiebreaker 14–12 to Nadal at the Rogers Cup in Montreal in 2008 was a heartbreaker, and since then he hadn't even been able to win a set against the Spaniard. The moment he sunk a backhand volley into the net on Nadal's third first-set point the game—and to all intents the match—was up. Forget advised him to go to the net more often after that in an attempt to disrupt Nadal's rhythm, but he just ended up getting passed at will. At least the end came mercifully quickly, as one hopes it does for the bulls here, with Gasquet beaten 6–3 6–0 6–1. Nadal's service figures couldn't have been more impressive: 100 percent on first- and second-serve points won.

All of which made it hard to believe two of the statements he made afterward: "I'm close to the end of my energy," he said. And, "If the match stays longer it would be very difficult for me."

Simon, it was hoped, would put up stiffer resistance. He had defeated David Ferrer the last time they met, just a month earlier, but that was on a hard court in Cincinnati. Their previous two meetings on clay had

comfortably gone Ferrer's way. "I know exactly what he's going to do," said Simon. "He's not changing his game, just playing right, left, right, left—he never lets you breathe one second. He's a real warrior."

Simon must have had a crystal ball, because that's exactly what happened. He was in contention in the second set, in which he broke Ferrer twice and had a further three break points to go 5–5. But once he had surrendered that set it just got, as he admitted, "harder and harder," and he eventually lost 6–1 6–4 6–1 in two

Pictured above (from left to right):
David Ferrer (ESP);
Michael Llodra (FRA) and
Jo-Wilfried Tsonga (FRA)

hours, eight minutes. That was one minute less than it had taken Nadal to dispatch Gasquet back to the welcome cool of the changing rooms. Asked about his indefatigable spirit afterward, Ferrer nodded in agreement and concurred with a smile that he was "like Rafa." There are clearly no egos in this Spanish camp.

On the eve of the opening day's singles, Forget said he would be smothering himself in SPF 30 sunblock and preparing for a long day's toil in the Andalusian sun. Although Albert Costa, the Spanish captain, sometimes resembled an overworked attendant in a Turkish bathhouse, dashing hither and thither with cold, wet towels to drape over his players' heads during changeovers, no one was in much danger of getting sunburned. Two best-of-five-set clay-court matches wrapped up inside four and a quarter hours was a real result for the Spanish in more ways than one.

Costa revealed afterward that he was "more worried about Rafa than David" after his exertions in New York and thought he had played an intelligent match in getting the job done so smartly. There were few crumbs of comfort for Forget.

"It's very painful to watch your players suffer on the court against such a good team," he said. "Some of the French journalists expected Nadal to be a little tired and to not be completely used to the clay, and he

did more than that. He just played as good as he can play when he plays at the French [Open]. And Richard, except for the first set, couldn't keep up with that level, physically or technically. In every aspect of the game Rafa was much better.

"Gilles, on the other hand, had some chances in the second set. He could have stayed with him, but David, again, was too good. They played alright but to beat Spain in Spain you have to play great, and that was not the case."

On day two France did play great to dispel any hopes the Spanish might have of winning the tie inside two days. In prospect, the doubles looked a close match, possibly even one that favored Spain since unlike Verdasco and Feliciano Lopez, Tsonga and Michael Llodra are not a recognized pairing; Tsonga, in fact, was Llodra's seventh Davis Cup doubles partner. But they served superbly and returned even better. "I've seen them a lot in practice and I can tell you it's by far the best I've seen them play," said Forget with brutal honesty.

The two Spanish left-handers didn't seem to complement each other at all and suffered a 6–1 6–2 6–0 defeat that was every bit as humiliating as the reverses endured by the French the previous day. According to Llodra, Forget had delivered "a good speech" beforehand and they went into the rubber strongly motivated. "After losing two points on the first day quite easily, we wanted to be proud to be French and we came to the court with big teeth," he said.

Tsonga's form seemed to justify the view of those who thought Forget had erred in leaving him out of the singles, and during the press conference afterward he strongly hinted to his captain that he would like the opportunity to square the tie against Nadal the next day, which was probably what Forget had always intended, anyway.

and it didn't take Tsonga long to appreciate that fact as Nadal got his own "big teeth" into the Frenchman from the start and refused to let go, Tsonga eventually surrendering his opening serve on the fourth break point. (He liked to think that things might have been different had he held in that game but it's doubtful.)

Not that Forget would have taken any pleasure in telling everyone "I told you so," but his reservations about Tsonga on clay were fully vindicated as the big man went down 6–0 6–2 6–4. Tsonga didn't win a

It was tempting, as it must have been for Tsonga, to recall the time he blew Nadal away at the 2008 Australian Open, but he had only beaten him once since then, during the summer at the Aegon Championships, which, of course, was on grass. Even if the improbable should happen, France would still need Gasquet to beat Ferrer in the final rubber—something he had managed to do just once in six attempts.

As usual, it was up to Forget to put things in perspective. "We still have to beat the best player in the world on clay in the last six years at home," he said. "It's not going to be easy. We still need a miracle."

Costa's warning that Nadal would be "much better" than on the opening day was equally ominous

single point on Nadal's serve in the first set and in mitigation claimed that even Roger Federer had trouble with the spin. Seventeen break points to Nadal and none to Tsonga said it all. He probably didn't need to hear the confirmation that followed from Costa: "When this guy plays good on clay he's unbeatable."

Nadal cannot have gone into the tie in the best frame of mind, just four days after losing his sixth final out of six in 2011 to Novak Djokovic. But, like the champion he is, he picked himself up to produce six sets of sublime tennis on his favorite surface to send Spain into its sixth final of the new millennium. Suddenly the number six, he must have thought, had a better ring to it. ●

Pictured above (from left to right):
David Ferrer (ESP);
Jo-Wilfried Tsonga (FRA);
Fernando Verdasco (ESP)

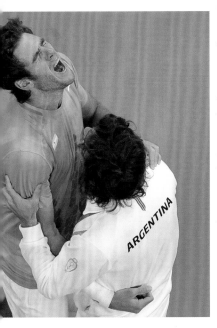

Serbia v Argentina

Tito Vazquez knew it, as did his opposite number, Bogdan Obradovic. The moment Novak Djokovic laid his hands on his first US Open trophy, he unknowingly released them on the Davis Cup. A bittersweet moment if ever there was for a great champion, and not least a great champion of Davis Cup.

Argentina's captain is a wily old bird, and he knew his country's best hope of beating the holders in their own backyard was if Serbia's No. 1 and world No. 1 triumphed in New York. As for Serbia's captain, he was left to bemoan the fact that the Arthur Ashe Stadium still doesn't have a roof to prevent the kind of overrun that this year's US Open experienced.

Djokovic, of course, had also gone as deep as possible into the tournament in 2010 when the final was also delayed one day by the rain, but the difference on that occasion, when he finished runner-up to Rafael Nadal, was that he caught the first plane back to Belgrade for the semifinal against Czech Republic. And even then he was considered not ready to play the opening-day singles rubbers. This time he was obliged to stay on a further two days to fulfill media commitments. On top of that, he was carrying injuries, which began during the US Open. It says much about the commitment of Djokovic to Davis Cup that he was in Belgrade at all.

"I thought, 'it's too much for the guy,' even though we know he's a gladiator," said Vazquez, who quite rightly chose not to dwell overly long on Serbia's misfortune after Djokovic was forced to retire in the crucial fourth rubber against Juan Martin del Potro. "It's a real happiness even though we are sad for Novak—the team likes the guy."

Argentina thoroughly deserved the plaudits and, moreover, it would have taken one of Djokovic's Herculean efforts rather than a mere gladiatorial one to have stopped del Potro in the form the big man was in. As he conceded: "I am not saying I would have won if I had been 100 percent fit because del Potro played at a very high level. Never in my professional career have I struggled with my return of serve as I did today."

Pictured clockwise from top left:

Juan Ignacio Chela (ARG)

and Juan Monaco (ARG);

Viktor Troicki (SRB) and

Nenad Zimonjic (SRB);

Argentina captain Tito Vazquez

Pictured opposite:

David Nalbandian (ARG)

Winning away from home has become second nature to Argentina these past two years, but that hasn't always been the case. The last time they visited Belgrade—forty-seven years ago—they were thrashed 5–0 by a Yugoslav team inspired by Niki Pilic, who up until last year had been advising the Serbian team. It was the only time Argentina and the old country ever met. No wonder that great Davis Cup stalwart David Nalbandian remarked after the Argentines had taken an unprecedented 2–0 lead on the opening day: "History—we're here to make it!"

Unlike Djokovic, neither del Potro nor Nalbandian were seriously delayed by events in New York since both went out in the third round. In taking Nadal to a first-set tiebreak (which he narrowly lost) in his third-round match, the twenty-nine-year-old Nalbandian proved he was in good shape (and he is enough of a handful in Davis Cup when in poor shape). The news that Djokovic was somewhere over the Atlantic when the draw pitted the two men against one another in the opening rubber was not about to shake his resolve.

Whether it was gamesmanship or wishful thinking on the part of the Serbian team to name Djokovic was difficult to determine. What was clear was Serbia's respect for the opposition, because until then they had not once during the year called on the services of their No. 1 in singles. It meant that under Davis Cup rules Djokovic, who landed less than twenty-four hours before the start of play, was committed to play unless his team could provide the referee with a sick note from the tie's independent doctor—either that or suffer an Argentine walkover in the opening rubber.

As for Argentina, it was in no position to hold back anyone. As per the old sporting cliché, it really was a case of them taking it one match at a time. "Every match is difficult in this tie, but every match counts, so we're going out from the beginning to put out the best that we have," said Vazquez.

As it transpired, the pain to Djokovic's lower back and ribs was too much for him to play on day one, and Viktor Troicki took his place. Nalbandian, who said he learned of the change about half an hour before the start, has been around too long to be affected by such matters, as was evident once the match began. Troicki, however, was the first to break, in the third game, but this failed to instill in him the confidence he needed to beat someone of Nalbandian's stature, and the Argentine, who led 3–1 in head-to-heads, broke back twice to take the first set.

As Vazquez said of his No. 2, sounding more like a football manager than a tennis captain, "he's a real cup player." Although Troicki then leveled it at one set all, the vastly more experienced Nalbandian was in the groove and got inspired rather than intimidated by the crowd of 15,000 in the Belgrade Arena. Not for the first time in recent years—nor probably the last—the world No. 74 made a mockery of the rankings, comfortably beating the world No. 16, 6–4 4–6 6–2 6–3.

This only added to the pressure then on Janko Tipsarevic in the second rubber against del Potro. Afterward, Serbia's No. 2 would say he had already heaped enough on himself with his resolve to sustain his recent good form. By reaching the semifinals of the Rogers Cup in Montreal and the quarterfinals of the US Open, he had achieved a career-high ranking of No. 13. It was felt that the low-bouncing, medium-fast surface of the Belgrade Arena would suit him, as he was the smaller man. So much for that theory.

Having saved four set points on his serve in the tenth game of the opening set, Tipsarevic then played what he described as a "stupid" game to forfeit his serve and the set. It's bad enough losing the opening set against anyone, but according to the Serb it's invariably fatal to do so against the Argentine, who proceeded to pummel Tipsarevic into submission. Del Potro described his 7–5 6–3 6–4 win as "one of my best of the season."

"Everybody knows when Juan Martin is leading he gets more confidence and starts to swing his forehand and serve better," said Tipsarevic, who blamed himself for playing too far back. "I feel the key to his victory was me not being able to get a hold of his serve. He was just serving too good and winning too many free points."

The Serb didn't help matters by committing fifty-one unforced errors, compared to his opponent's twenty-four. He consoled himself with the thought that he would make amends in the reverse singles, but would he get the chance to do so? Defeat inside two days at a venue where they had never before been beaten in five ties was unthinkable for the Serbs. The question was, would "Super Novak," if fit, be introduced into their doubles lineup? Such a tactic had backfired on them badly twelve months earlier when they played the Czech Republic, but in that tie they were all square after the first day's play and could just about afford to lose the doubles.

As it turned out, they decided to give Djokovic one more day's rest and put their trust in the Nenad Zimonjic–Troicki axis. It was a wise decision because the Serbian pair proved much too good for their opponents, Juan Monaco and Juan Ignacio Chela, winning 7–6(4) 6–4 6–2. The Argentines briefly threatened to make a match of it when they broke Zimonjic to take a 4–1 lead in the second set, only for the Serbs to win eleven of the remaining thirteen games.

"It was a must-win situation for us. We were definitely under pressure and we played really well under the circumstances," said Zimonjic.

He felt that in the first set Troicki was still suffering from the aftereffects of the singles when the confidence he usually enjoys in the Belgrade Arena temporarily deserted him. But with the help of the world No. 3 doubles player—who Troicki said was like an older brother to him—he gradually recovered that feel-good factor that was famously evident in the deciding rubber against France in last year's final.

Pictured below (from left to right):
Janko Tipsarevic (SRB);
Juan Martin del Potro (ARG)

Pictured above (from left to right):

Viktor Troicki (SRB) and

Novak Djokovic (SRB);

The Argentine team celebrates

"Every second on this court and in this arena gets me back to the final in 2010 against [Michael] Llodra and always gives me confidence when I play here," said Troicki.

In the confident expectation that Djokovic, who had not been beaten in a singles rubber since losing to Nadal on clay in March 2009, would now pick up the gauntlet, Zimonjic observed: "I like our chances." It made a little more sense than Obradovic's obscure grasp of arithmetic: "Now we are equal," estimated the Serbian captain.

Del Potro was obviously looking forward to the matchup with Djokovic despite having lost all four of their prior meetings. Djokovic, however, never played del Potro during his purple patch in the second half of 2009, when he won the US Open, and which he now seemed to be returning to. "It's not often you play the No. 1 in his house," said the Argentine with obvious relish.

When the new US Open champion walked out on court to a hero's welcome from the 15,000-strong crowd it momentarily seemed that that alone might be enough to carry him to victory. Del Potro, however, has no respect for reputations—nor wounded opponents— and his serve was soon working as ruthlessly as it had against Tipsarevic. Djokovic went toe-to-toe with him for thirteen games, but it was evident that anything

less than 100 percent—and he was clearly substantially less than that—was not going to get the job done.

At 7–6(5) 3–0 down he let out a painful scream and collapsed to the floor before being helped to the bench by his teammates and captain. It was only his third defeat in sixty-six matches and one in mitigating circumstances at that. No wonder he limped from the court to the same sort of applause as that which greeted him.

Djokovic accepted full responsibility for the gamble, even though such decisions are usually made by the team as a whole (they are a democratic lot the Serbians). However, given that Troicki's chances of victory were slim to zero against del Potro in this kind of form, the only real gamble was to Djokovic's health, and that thankfully didn't suffer unduly.

"We knew my condition was not good but we believed that even so I would have a better chance against del Potro than my teammate Viktor Troicki," he said. "It was my decision and it backfired."

But there were no regrets. As Djokovic said: "We were champions in 2010, we've played semifinals this year, what more can you ask of a small nation?"

In fact, they ask quite a lot of themselves, and Djokovic and his teammates desperately want to challenge Spain's hegemony in this competition, but that must be left to another year—and, for the time being, another country. ●

Patrick McEnroe

In his ten years as captain of the United States team, Patrick McEnroe lost just one match at home, and it resulted in his biggest regret. With Andre Agassi back in the fold, Andy Roddick in his prime, and the Bryan brothers already established as the best doubles team in the world, McEnroe had good reason in 2005 to feel confident about their chances. But in Davis Cup it's never a good idea to get ahead of oneself, and USA fell flat on its face at the first hurdle.

It was due partly to a mistake the young captain had made in his choice of surface and partly to the excellence of the "two-man" Croatian team (some might say the one-man team of Ivan Ljubicic). McEnroe had laid a surface that was "a little too slow for Agassi, and he didn't like it." Like all good captains, he didn't make the same mistake twice, and two years later he realized his dream of winning the Davis Cup on a surface at Portland, Oregon, that was uncomfortably quick for the Russians.

"Here's what's amazing about Davis Cup—for a country like us you can just as easily lose in the first round as win the whole thing," he said.

It was a little ironic that his brother John had resigned the captaincy after just fourteen months in

charge, largely due to frustration at his inability to persuade Agassi (and Pete Sampras) to commit to Davis Cup. Patrick's success in that area may have been short-lived, but there is no doubt that having spent his playing career in the shadow of his famous older brother, he stepped out of it once he became captain.

Taking charge of a group of players not much younger than himself—he was just thirty-four—called for a wise head on young shoulders, and in McEnroe the USTA found one. He quickly realized something his brother had had a problem grasping, which is that frustration in getting players to play was "misguided."

"It is the beast that it is, and you have to deal with it," he said. "If you're in a position where you're begging players to play, they're probably not going to play their best, anyway. I was lucky that I got [Andy] Roddick, [James] Blake, and the Bryans at a time when they were all very young, very eager to play and got along well with each other."

Sensitivity with regards to the specific demands of each player was of paramount importance. He remembered what his tennis coach at Stanford, Dick Gould, had told him: "You don't necessarily treat everybody the same—in fact you probably don't—but you treat them all fairly."

"The main thing," said McEnroe "is to understand your players, knowing during matches when to talk and, most importantly, when not to talk. Someone like Roddick, who is very clear-minded about what he wants to do—sometimes for better or worse—listens to everything you say, and if you say something he doesn't agree with he might tune me out for a while.

"Whereas the Bryan brothers wanted to hear the most basic things repeated to them every changeover. And then Blake, the way he played, going for broke, he'd make your hair turn gray or want to pull it out. But you had to work with that and get the best out of him."

McEnroe knew from his own playing days that there were some things about Davis Cup you cannot teach or advise on. "I was lucky enough to play Davis Cup a few times, in doubles, and someone said to me, 'You must have talked to your brother, he must have helped you.' And I said, 'No, he didn't help me a lick,'

but I realized when I went out there and played, nothing can really prepare you for that. The difference in hearing, 'Game, United States' and the pressure of playing for your country and your teammates is really unique."

McEnroe was captain of the U.S. team longer than anyone else in the team's history and was proud of what they achieved. They had excellent singles players and a great doubles team, even if in an ideal world he would have had someone like his brother who could play singles and doubles—"certainly the positives of having the Bryans outweighed the negatives." All they lacked were versatile players, which McEnroe is now attempting to address in his new role as the General Manager of USTA Player Development.

Versatility is a quality that future American teams may possess if the success of young Bjorn Fratangelo at the 2011 Junior French Open is anything to go by, and McEnroe believes that nineteen-year-old US Open mixed doubles champion Jack Sock could make a good clay court player in the Spanish mold if he got himself in great condition.

"We won a final, we made a couple of semis, but we still didn't beat a powerhouse team on the road," he said. "Anytime other countries play the U.S. at home they're going to put down the slowest clay court possible. Versatility—that's the biggest challenge for us." ●

THE FIFTH MAN

A passionate crowd is part of what makes Davis Cup so special, and there's nothing quite like the sound of thousands of vocal fans chanting a player's name to help give him a much-needed boost.

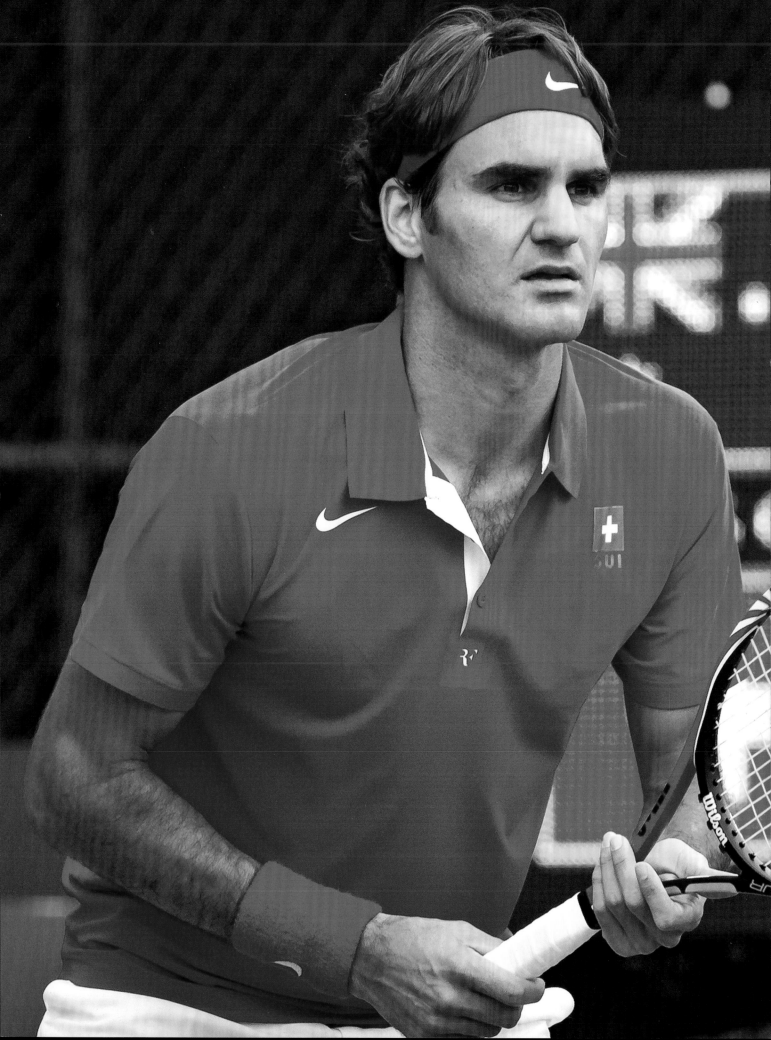

Play-offs 16–18 September

		Switzerland defeated Australia 3–2	SYDNEY, AUSTRALIA—OUTDOOR GRASS
		Italy defeated Chile 4–1	SANTIAGO, CHILE—OUTDOOR HARD
		Canada defeated Israel 3–2	RAMAT HASHARON, ISRAEL—OUTDOOR HARD
		Croatia defeated South Africa 4–1	POTCHEFSTROOM, SOUTH AFRICA—OUTDOOR HARD
		Russia defeated Brazil 3–2	KAZAN, RUSSIA—INDOOR HARD
		Austria defeated Belgium 4–1	ANTWERP, BELGIUM—INDOOR HARD
		Japan defeated India 4–1	TOKYO, JAPAN—OUTDOOR HARD
		Czech Republic defeated Romania 5–0	BUCHAREST, ROMANIA—OUTDOOR CLAY

Introduction

One way or another, old favorites dominated the talk in the World Group play-off round. Whenever Davis Cup comes calling, it seems the likes of Lleyton Hewitt, Radek Stepanek, and Mikhail Youzhny manage to produce their best—no matter the state of their form or health. It's no coincidence that all three have a great pedigree in the competition.

Sadly, not all of those who have served Davis Cup faithfully and well were able to do themselves justice. One of the game's most popular players, thirty-one-year-old Fernando Gonzalez, broke down in Chile's tie against Italy in Santiago following a recent hip operation, while his longtime partner and fellow Olympic gold medalist Nicolas Massu was also unable to finish his rubber.

Hewitt, aged thirty, has had one of the worst seasons of his career for injury and yet very nearly managed to hold it together over three rubbers to pull off an improbable victory against Switzerland, eventually losing a fifth and final rubber, spread over two days, to Stanislas Wawrinka. His record against the great Roger Federer says it all: six wins out of twenty-three in normal tournament play; two wins out of three in Davis Cup.

The thirty-three-year-old Stepanek had managed to revive his ranking in 2011, but even when it has plummeted in recent years he has come alive in Davis Cup. Once again he was responsible for firing Czech Republic to victory, against Romania. Clearly he is driven by the search for that elusive Davis Cup triumph that would round off his career just perfectly.

Players like Hewitt and Youzhny have already lifted Dwight Davis's trophy—in Hewitt's case on two occasions—but still they want more.

The bonus is that such enthusiasm and commitment rubs off on the young men around them and this play-off round surely produced Davis Cup stars of the future in Canada's Vasek Pospisil, who contributed three points in his country's 3-2 win in Israel and Japan's Yuichi Sugita, who even outshone Kei Nishikori in the Land of the Rising Sun's 4-1 triumph over India. ●

Australia v Switzerland

There is always a sense of anticlimax in the denouement of a cliffhanger, and the play-off between Australia and Switzerland at the Royal Sydney Golf Club was no different. The three minutes it took to resolve the outcome was almost irrelevant when set beside what had gone before. This tie will be remembered for what happened rather than who won and for the courage and commitment of its leading combatants.

When it comes to those qualities, we expect nothing less from Lleyton Hewitt. The two-time grand slam champion has been one of the game's great warriors, but at thirty years of age and towards the end of a year ravaged by injury, the Australian has to finally accept he is a mere mortal. And yet he produced a level of performance that made a mockery of his No. 199 ranking and defied anyone to write him off just yet. No wonder his captain Pat Rafter called him "a freak."

Twice a set up in what was surprisingly his first-ever live fifth rubber, Australia's most successful Davis Cup player found himself trailing 5–3 in the fifth set to

Stanislas Wawrinka when the referee Javier Moreno, of Spain, halted play because of fading light. This understandably caused an uproar, less about the decision than the timing of it—six minutes past the scheduled finish of 5:45 p.m.

Rafter had complained to Moreno several times about the conditions, and when the match was halted it left Hewitt one break down and in the tricky position of having to serve first the following morning. Even though he took a 30–0 lead when play resumed, it was obvious that, with his right knee heavily taped, his movement was limited and he was obliged to go for winners.

Unable to push off properly on his right leg, he served two consecutive double faults before two errant forehands handed the rubber and tie to Switzerland, Wawrinka winning 4–6 6–4 6–7(7) 6–4 6–3 in just over four hours.

The Swiss was no less courageous, having played throughout on painkillers for a leg injury not to mention a grass surface that was "for sure" not his best. In all the excitement, it was almost forgotten that Roger Federer was part of this tie and a rather significant part, too, since he won both his singles rubbers. But according to the sixteen-time grand slam champion it was Wawrinka who was "heroic."

Federer could sympathize with the Australians, having twice lost grand slam finals himself in darkness. "It's the worst feeling in the world to lose in conditions you shouldn't be playing in," he remarked.

The world No. 4 was happy to be cheerleader during that final rubber. As he said after beating

eighteen-year-old Bernard Tomic 6–2 7–5 3–6 6–3 to square the tie at two all on the Sunday: "If Stan wants me to do push-ups to pump him up, I'll do that. If he wants me to sleep on the floor of his bedroom, to keep him warm as we're both missing our children... whatever he wants me to do."

It showed how much the Davis Cup meant to him that he was in Australia so soon after his cruel loss to Novak Djokovic at the US Open. It's the only piece of worthwhile silverware he hasn't lifted (and on evidence of this tie, don't bet on that remaining so). One has only to recall his celebration when he and Wawrinka won the gold medal in the doubles at the Beijing Olympics to realize how much he values the esprit de corps.

No one should have been too surprised when young Tomic—who went from qualifier to quarterfinalist at Wimbledon—beat the higher-ranked Wawrinka 4–6 6–4 6–3 6–3 in the opening rubber, or when Federer beat Hewitt for the eighteenth time in twenty-six meetings, 5–7 7–6(5) 6–2 6–3, to square the tie.

For a man who produced his greatest comeback against Federer in Davis Cup, when coming from two sets and 5–2 down to beat the world No. 1 in Melbourne eight years earlier, coming back to win the doubles was a minor feat. Nevertheless, doubles great Todd Woodbridge thought his and Chris Guccione's 2–6 6–4 6–2 7–6(5) victory against the Olympic champions was "one of the best doubles performances in Australia's Davis Cup history".

Ultimately, the final rubber proved a match too far for Hewitt—but not by much. ●

Pictured clockwise from top left:
Roger Federer (SUI);
Bernard Tomic (AUS);
Stanislas Wawrinka (SUI)

Pictured clockwise from top left:

Simone Bolelli (ITA) celebrates

with his team; Paul Capdeville (CHI);

Fernando Gonzalez (CHI)

Chile v Italy

A return to the halcyon days of the 1970s may be a long way off for Italian tennis, but winning their first World Group play-off in five attempts was a step in the right direction. It was probably just coincidental, but their 4–1 win took place at the Stadio Nacional in Santiago, which was where Italy won the Davis Cup for the only time in its history in 1976, also 4–1. It won't have meant much to the players, but it meant a lot to Corrado Barazzutti, the Italian captain, who was a member of the team that won that final.

Hans Gildemeister, the Chilean captain, was the non-playing fifth member of the opposition team, and other players from the tie were present for this play-off. Nostalgia hung heavily in the air, since the outcome of this tie may also have signaled the end of an era for Chilean tennis. Fernando Gonzalez, their hugely popular No. 1, who has been trying to re-establish himself after hip surgery, broke down in the second rubber, and then in the final rubber their struggling two-time Olympic champion, Nicolas Massu, retired.

It is players of their caliber—and that of Adriano Panatta, who led Italy to that Davis Cup triumph and three further finals—that Italy has lacked during the past three decades. Not for the first time their legendary Davis Cup player, Nicolas Pietrangeli, bemoaned the lack of a big champion around whom a team could be built. Italy may have to be patient a little while longer. In fact, it could be that their wait will be as long as that of Chile, whose youngsters won the 2010 world under-14 title in Prostejov by defeating Italy in the final.

Gonzalez was absent when Chile lost 4–1 at home to the United States in the first round in March. During the summer he was out for three months following hip surgery to cure a troublesome knee. During his comeback he played six events, of which only three were at tour level, and twice he had to retire. So it was with some trepidation that Chilean fans watched him face off against Fabio Fognini, a quarterfinalist at the French Open.

Nevertheless, even Barazzutti expected him to square the tie after Paul Capdeville lost the opening rubber to Potito Starace 6–3 6–3 2–6 7–6(5). "Gonzo" started sluggishly but looked much more like his old self in the second set, winding up that monstrous forehand of his and serving well. Even so, his mobility remained poor and then early in the third set he collapsed in pain. The doctor was called, but after attempting to continue he was forced to retire with the score at 6–2 4–6 2–1 in Fognini's favor.

He was already on his way to the hospital to discover the extent of the microtear in his left leg when his captain spoke for him. "Fernando is in deep pain" said Gildemeister, "not only because of the physical problem, but also because of what goes on in his mind and heart."

After that, an Italian victory was a formality, and Fognini and Simone Bolelli, who had just reached the semifinals of the US Open, were not about to miss the opportunity, beating Massu and Jorge Aguilar 6–4 6–4 6–4. "We know that Fernando Gonzalez's injury had a big impact in this series, and we expected more difficulties, but we are very happy to have won [through] to the Serie A of tennis," said Fognini.

There will have been little consolation for Chile in Capdeville's 7–6(3) 6–2 victory over Bolelli in the first of the dead rubbers and only further misery in the

second when Massu, who had been struggling all year with form and fitness, was forced to retire with an abdominal injury while trailing Daniele Bracciali 4–3. But Massu, for one, was not about to wallow in self-pity. "This is a sport of men, and men do not cry when they lose," he said. "They were better than us in the court and that's it." ●

Pictured above (from left to right):
Potito Starace (ITA);
Nicolas Massu (CHI)

Israel v Canada

Despite its excellent home record, the omens weren't good for Israel receiving Canada at a venue called the Canada Stadium in Ramat Hasharon. Any advantage the visitors might have had, though, was offset by the fact that their No. 1, Milos Raonic—comfortably the highest-ranked player in the tie at No. 31—was still recuperating from a hip injury. Had the Israelis known that he also had a virus they might have approached this tie in a more positive frame of mind.

What they definitely hadn't bargained for was the performance of the Canadian No. 2, Vasek Pospisil, who went on to contribute all the points in Canada's 3–2 win, which put them back in the World Group for the first time in seven years. Amir Weintraub, the man he beat in the decisive rubber, described him as "the joker in the Canadian pack."

Pictured clockwise from above:

Vasek Pospisil (CAN);

Dudi Sela (ISR);

Amir Weintraub (ISR)

Had anyone done their homework on the twenty-one-year-old they would have discovered that he was more like the ace in the pack than the joker. He had just come through qualifying to make the main draw of the US Open, where he lost in the second round in four fiercely fought sets to No. 25 seed, Feliciano Lopez, of Spain. And prior to that he had taken none other than Roger Federer—his idol—to a close opening set in Montreal.

Therefore, he had nothing to fear against Dudi Sela in the opening rubber, even if the Israeli was higher ranked and, of course, a lot more experienced. Eyal Ran's team was unbeaten in six of their last eight home ties, but Sela was unable to tap into the crowd's passionate support, and Pospisil, who played with the composure of a veteran according to his captain, Martin Laurendeau, went on to win 7–6(4) 6–7(6) 6–1 6–7(2) 6–3 in five hours.

"Playing Davis Cup is an honor," said Pospisil. "To play in a huge match like this against a great player and win my first five-set match like this ... it's just an incredible feeling."

And there was much more to come from him. In normal circumstances, Raonic could have been expected to give Canada a 2–0 lead, but he clearly wasn't right and faded in the humid evening air against the twenty-fifth-birthday boy Weintraub, who was ranked 151 places beneath him, losing 5–7 7–5 6–3 6–1.

Laurendeau revealed afterward that Raonic had gone to the hospital suffering from a virus thirty-six hours before the tie and had stayed in bed for the best part of two days. Although more or less recovered from the hip injury, he hadn't hit a competitive ball since Wimbledon three months earlier.

"It was important for him to use this match as a reference and go from here," said Laurendeau. "It was a good effort on his part, but kudos for Weintraub on his birthday ... ultimately Milos is no superhuman."

Israel was beginning to think that Pospisil was, though. The next day he and Daniel Nestor pulled off a momentous victory in the doubles when they beat the crack pairing of Andy Ram and Jonathan Erlich 4–6 6–3 6–4 6–4. It was the first time the Israelis had lost a Davis Cup rubber at home since March 2005, when the unheralded British duo of Andy Murray and David Sherwood defeated them, and they fended off four match points here before eventually succumbing.

The withdrawal of the Montenegro-born Raonic meant there was a huge discrepancy in the rankings of the two players contesting the fourth rubber. Sela—ranked No. 96—defeated Peter Polansky—ranked No. 573—about as easily as the 6–3 6–3 6–3 scoreline and rankings suggested.

The stage was then set for Pospisil to complete his one-man show. Only fatigue could stop him now, but he was on a high and made it across the finish line with something to spare as he beat Weintraub 6–2 7–6(3) 6–4.

"Pospisil made it hard for all of us—he came and took this tie all by himself," said Weintraub generously. "He was playing amazing: big returns, unbelievable serving, especially when he was tired he came every time on important points, and he deserves all the applause."

Canada has two very promising singles players born in 1990 and still a year or two left in the legs of Nestor, ranked No. 5 in doubles. We may find that the threat from North America in the future bears the Maple Leaf rather than the Stars and Stripes. ●

South Africa
v Croatia

The job facing South Africa was difficult enough without losing their No. 1, Kevin Anderson, before the start of play on the third day against Croatia. They were looking to the big server from Johannesburg playing on all three days if they were to have any chance against the former champions and had already lost him for the doubles. With Izak van der Merwe retiring with a wrist injury in the second rubber, it was as much as South Africa could do to limp across the finish line, never mind win the race.

Anderson was in good form going into the tie and had beaten world No. 4, Andy Murray, in straight sets at the Rogers Cup in Montreal just a month earlier. So it was not unreasonable to hope that he could take two points in the singles against Marin Cilic and Ivan Dodig on a fast outdoor court at the Fanie du Toit Sports Stadium in Potchefstroom. The state of his form—if not his health—was further underlined a fortnight after the tie, when he beat the former world No. 1, Andy Roddick, in straight sets in Beijing.

But after duly defeating Dodig 6–3 6–4 3–6 7–6(5), albeit with heavy strapping to his left leg, in the opening rubber he was forced to pull out of the doubles. Goran Prpic, the Croatian captain, assumed it was purely precautionary because he had watched Anderson practice in the morning on the Saturday and thought he

Pictured clockwise from above:
Kevin Anderson (RSA);
Milos Raonic (CAN);
Jonathan Erlich (ISR)
and Andy Ram (ISR);
Daniel Nestor (CAN)
and Vasek Pospisil (CAN)

looked "okay." He was as surprised as anyone when Anderson then withdrew from the reverse singles also.

"I woke up on Sunday thinking I could play, but the hip was still pretty sore and I was struggling [to move]," Anderson said. "I went out there on Friday and played my best tennis, but then I tweaked my hip pretty badly. I took a break from the doubles on Saturday, thinking that the rest will help me to get back on Sunday, but it didn't work out."

Rik de Voest took his place in what was expected to be the critical rubber, against Cilic, and was soundly beaten 6–4 6–2 6–4 to hand Croatia the tie. Frustratingly, John Laffnie de Jager, South Africa's captain, was left wondering "if only," because even without Anderson in the doubles, South Africa had its chances: thirteen of them to be exact, but it managed to break just once.

Croatia is still struggling to come to terms with life without Ivan Ljubicic and Mario Ancic, the men who had carried them to the title in 2005. Cilic's very promising career had suffered a few setbacks in the previous twelve months and now, instead of knocking on the door of the Top 10, he was struggling to break back into the Top 20. Dodig, on the other hand, had moved up one hundred places in the rankings in the past year to No. 37.

However, he looked no match for the similarly ranked Anderson early in that opening rubber. By the time Dodig got a handle—almost literally—on Anderson's booming serve it was too late.

Van der Merwe had been something of a surprise choice for the second spot. He and the more experienced de Voest have similar rankings but de Jager felt he needed to fight fire with fire (or rather firepower with firepower), and since van der Merwe was the bigger server of the two he went with him. Unfortunately for South Africa, van der Merwe awoke on the morning of the match feeling discomfort in his wrist, and after fifty-one minutes of play, with the score 6–0 6–0 to Cilic, he was forced to retire. He expected a six-week layoff.

Anderson and de Voest had won their only Davis Cup match together a couple of months earlier against the Netherlands, whereas de Voest and Raven Klaasen were completely untried. They put up a decent fight against Cilic and Dodig and might have done even better had they converted a few more of those break point chances, but their 6–2 6–4 3–6 6–1 defeat handed Croatia the initiative, which it never surrendered. ●

Pictured clockwise from above:

Marin Cilic (CRO);

Croatian fans;

Ivan Dodig (CRO) and

Marin Cilic (CRO);

Rik de Voest (RSA)

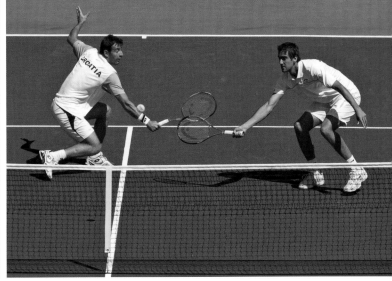

Russia v Brazil

Few players in the world know better than Mikhail Youzhny what it's like to come back from the brink in Davis Cup. The Russian did so most memorably in the 2002 Davis Cup final when, at the age of twenty, he came back from two sets to love down to win the fifth and final rubber against France's Paul-Henri Mathieu, prompting Marat Safin to describe Russia's first-ever title success as "better than sex."

Nine years later, Youzhny, the elder statesman of the Russian team who had come out of Davis Cup retirement to contest this tie, showed he had lost none of his nerve as he twice fended off a match point against Brazil's Thomaz Bellucci that, if conceded, would have condemned Russia to its first relegation from the World Group in twenty-two years. Again his teammates rallied around, just as they had in Paris all those years before when defeat stared them in the face, enabling Youzhny to pick himself up and go on to claim a famous victory, by 2–6 6–3 5–7 6–4 14–12, in a match lasting five hours.

It's a wonder it didn't leave his cheerleader, Dmitry Tursunov, emotionally drained for the deciding rubber, which he only knew he would be playing—instead of Igor Andreev—about fifteen minutes beforehand. When it comes to coolness, the blond-haired Russian makes Steve McQueen look like a nervous wreck—and he's another man who knows a thing or two about great escapes. Treating it like any other match, Tursunov went on to beat Ricardo Mello 6–1 7–6(5) 2–6 6–3 to preserve Russia's World Group status for another year.

"I didn't look at it as how big the pressure was," said Tursunov, whom many will remember outlasting the American Andy Roddick in a marathon final set to put Russia into the 2006 final. "I knew there were only two possible results: I'm either going to win or I'm going to lose. Neither one of these results was going to be career-ending, life-ending; it's not going to end our team existence. There's no point in beating yourself up."

Afterward Tursunov was at pains to explain his extrovert behavior during Youzhny's match. "I was trying to pump up Mikhail—he likes that sort of stuff, a bit of screaming and the crowd getting behind him," he said. "In that first set I thought we've really got to help him somehow. Thomaz was playing kind of ruthlessly. He seemed like he was playing without fear. Mikhail was a little bit more tentative, so we were trying to get him more aggressive.

"We hoped with all the noise and the commotion Thomaz would start treating it as 'Hey, wait a second, it's actually Davis Cup, there's a little bit of pressure here.' So hopefully the Brazilian team will not take it as a personal insult because it wasn't intended as that. It was simply to help our player."

Bellucci did not take offense and thought the crowd at the Kazan Tennis Academy—the only specialized tennis venue in the country—was "very respective" of all the players. "I've played some places much worse than here," he said. It was only the second time since 1994 that Russia had played a home tie outside of Moscow.

Pictured clockwise from top left:
Mikhail Youzhny (RUS);
Thomaz Bellucci (BRA);
Dmitry Tursunov (RUS)

The small pocket of Brazilian fans, which included the Brazilian ambassador and his wife, gave a good account of themselves, particularly when Bellucci beat a demoralized Andreev 6–4 6–3 6–3 to level the tie after Mello had found Youzhny "on another level" in losing 6–0 6–2 6–1. It was only to be expected, as was the whole of the first two days' play. Indeed Shamil Tarpischev, who has seen it all in his thirty-four years as Russia's captain, said on the eve of the tie: "It would be fair to assume we'll be tied after that opening Friday, and I don't think anyone would call that a bold prediction."

He could easily have added that Brazil would be leading 2–1 after the second day's play, because the 6–4 7–5 6–2 victory by Marcelo Melo and Bruno Soares over Tursunov and Igor Kunitsyn was also a given; the Brazilians are well-known doubles specialists, unlike their opponents. It was only then that this tie took on more of an unpredictable nature, producing a classic turnaround in fortunes. ●

Pictured (from left to right):
Ricardo Mello (BRA);
Marcelo Melo (BRA) and
Bruno Soares (BRA);
Austria captain Gilbert Schaller

Belgium v Austria

When Xavier Malisse—not for the first time in his career—beat Jurgen Melzer in straight sets at Wimbledon, the Belgians must have been feeling rather confident about their upcoming play-off against Austria, particularly since their No. 2, Steve Darcis, also had a winning record against the Austrian No. 1. Furthermore, of course, the tie was at home in Antwerp.

Had they also known that Darcis would repeat his victory three-and-a-half years earlier against Melzer on day one, Johan van Herck, Belgium's new captain, not unreasonably, would have anticipated starting life in his new job in the World Group. In Davis Cup, however, nothing can be taken for granted. In the space of three months, Malisse's confidence completely deserted him, while, in the space of three days, Melzer rediscovered his poise.

It was the outgoing Austrian captain, Gilbert Schaller, rather than the incoming Belgian one who finished the tie with a smile on his face. For the fifth time in five meetings dating back to 1933, the Austrians had beaten the Belgians. Schaller could ride off into the sunset safe in the knowledge that he had handed the team over to his successor in good shape.

"We have players coming through—which is important—and we're strong in doubles with different combinations," he said. "We have a bigger team now, including players such as Martin Fischer and Julian Knowle. When I took over the team, we had three or four players."

95

Malisse's summer started going wrong once he arrived in the United States for the start of the hard-court season. He lost his first match at each of the five tournaments he played there, although he was generally beaten by good men. That is not to say that Andreas Haider-Maurer isn't, but he is a lot less experienced. Even so, the Austrian, playing only his second Davis Cup rubber, won easily at 6–4 6–4 7–5.

Malisse's performance was even worse than the result—so bad, in fact, that it was obvious there was no way van Herck could risk him in the reverse rubber. "It was just horrible," said Malisse. "I couldn't put balls in the court. All he had to do was make two or three shots and then I made mistakes. It's been like this all summer."

At least Melzer had an excuse for his poor showing. He and the German Philipp Petzschner had been surprise winners of the men's doubles at the US Open the previous weekend, and he arrived in Belgium via Vienna suffering from jetlag and general fatigue. The world No. 21 took his lethargy onto the court and paid the price, losing to Darcis, ranked 72 places beneath him, 7–6(3) 6–7(4) 6–4 6–3.

"I was here for three days to prepare after six weeks in the States, but that's not an excuse," he said. "Steve played a great game, and you've got to give him credit. There will be criticism in the newspapers tomorrow, but I gave my best and will try to do better on Sunday."

Austria could afford to rest its grand slam doubles champion in the doubles rubber and still be assured of victory, Oliver Marach and Alexander Peya proving too good for Olivier Rochus and Darcis in a 6–4 3–6 6–4 6–4 win. As expected, Malisse was left out of the reverse singles.

"The way he played on Friday, we knew it was impossible to make him play on Sunday," said van Herck. "Xavier plays a lot on feelings. He needs to feel well. He didn't feel well at all, so he didn't have to tell me [he couldn't play]. We knew his weekend was over."

The little magician, Rochus, took his place against Melzer. The two men have had some close matches over the years, including a five-setter in Davis Cup eight years ago that Melzer just managed to win. But at thirty-one, Rochus is losing his magic and is no longer a match for the much-improved Austrian, who replaced his fourteen double faults in the second rubber with eleven aces in a tidy 6–4 6–4 6–3 victory that won the day. Hopefully, the newspaper reports will have reflected that. ●

Pictured clockwise from above:
Jurgen Melzer (AUT);
Andreas Haider-Maurer (AUT);
Xavier Malisse (BEL)

Japan v India

The absence of Leander Paes and an opening-rubber injury that ruled Somdev Devvarman out of the rest of the tie were clearly factors in India's 4–1 defeat to Japan, but nothing should be allowed to detract from the promise shown by the young Japanese team.

It made a pleasant change for their No. 1, Kei Nishikori, not to have to carry the burden of responsibility. That was happily removed from his

but not anymore. We are looking to the younger players going forward, especially in the doubles."

Paes, who injured his back in a mixed doubles match at the US Open, did not travel to Japan. As it turned out, India was still good enough to win the doubles. What was more damaging to India's chances was the injury to Devvarman, although when he called for a timeout to receive treatment to his right shoulder he was already trailing Sugita by two sets to love.

shoulders by Yuichi Sugita, who went into this tie as the host nation's lowest-ranked singles player. It was hoped Japan's No. 2 would extend Devvarman in the opening rubber, but instead he ended up beating him in straight sets. It's not often that Nishikori wins both his singles rubbers and is not the star of the show at the Ariake Coliseum in Tokyo.

Sugita is just two years older than Nishikori, having turned twenty-three on the final day of the tie, and impressed everyone with his level of performance, which was crucial to Japan moving back into the World Group for the first time since 1985. The accent now is clearly on youth in the Japanese setup, as Eiji Takeuchi, their captain, confirmed.

"We are aiming to create a talented pool of younger players," he said. "When I first took over as captain, the average age of our players was over thirty,

Sugita, who is ranked 110 places beneath Devvarman at No. 174, went on to win 6–3 6–4 7–5, and there could not have been a more popular winner. He hails from the area closest to the epicenter of the March 11 disaster in Japan. "I saw people from Sendai cheering for me in the crowd today and felt very emotional," he said. "I didn't play any differently than normal, but I did prepare for this match for one month and tried to envision my opponent."

Apart from scoring a much-needed point for Japan, this enabled Nishikori to go out and swing with no fear. In beating Rohan Bopanna 6–3 6–2 6–2, he didn't allow his opponent a single break point. The Indian, who is a doubles specialist, was sportingly fulsome in his praise of the world No. 55, saying: "He is playing at a high level. He is really quick. I think he is playing like a Top 30 player. He was fantastic."

Bopanna was relieved to get back into his comfort zone of doubles play the next day when, standing in for Paes, he and Mahesh Bhupathi beat Sugita and Tatsuma Ito 7–5 3–6 6–3 7–6(4). The Japanese pair had spent just two weeks practicing together and yet almost took the rubber to a fifth set against two players who are both in the world's Top 10. Sugita and Ito led 5–2 in the fourth but then lost four of the next five games. Even Bhupathi had to admit it "got a bit dicey."

It was revealed that Devvarman had attended a Tokyo hospital on the Saturday morning to be treated for a deltoid muscle strain, so it was no surprise to learn that he had been replaced in the reverse singles. Given Nishikori's form, the Japanese may well have been too strong for him, fit or otherwise. Nishikori certainly should have been far too strong for his replacement, Vishnu Vardhan, who was ranked No. 456 in the world, and yet the twenty-four-year-old made him work hard for his 7–5 6–3 6–3 victory, which clinched the tie.

Like Japan, India needs to start looking toward more youthful players, and All India Tennis Association vice president Karti Chidambaram admitted as much. "We need more guys like Vishnu. We will have a big hole to fill when Leander and Bhupathi retire." ●

Romania v Czech Republic

Czech Republic has produced some very fine players during the last three decades, but none in the men's game, apart from Ivan Lendl who defected in the mid-1980s, to rival the best from Sweden and United States. And yet they share with those two countries the proud record of only once slipping out of the World Group since its formation in 1981. It is an extraordinary achievement.

By surprisingly losing at home to Kazakhstan last March, that record was at risk when Czech Republic was drawn to play away against Romania in the play-offs. Ordinarily, the Czechs should be able to go to places such as Bucharest with a depleted team and still win, but there is no accounting for the part pressure can play in Davis Cup, and they kept their fingers crossed that their old warhorse, Radek Stepanek, would be fit for duty.

The thirty-two-year-old had missed the tie against Kazakhstan because of illness, although given his form at the time, there is no guarantee he would have made a difference. Since then, as luck would have it, he had rediscovered some of his old flair during the North American hard court season. He beat a strong field to win the Washington tournament and might have gone

Pictured clockwise from the top:
Tomas Berdych (CZE);
Marius Copil (ROU);
Yuichi Sugita (JPN)

a little bit—but that little bit makes a big difference. They have to start to believe, and work a little harder for what they want."

When a team records a whitewash as the Czechs went on to do, dropping just one set in the process, it's hard to believe that there were any "sweaty moments." And yet there were, according to one member of the Czech camp. Jaroslav Navratil, the captain, revealed that Berdych was, in fact, close to defaulting. Like Stepanek, he had finished the US Open with a shoulder injury and hadn't been able to practice much in the days leading up to the tie.

There was one more hiccup in the Czechs' performance, and that was when Berdych and Stepanek, who have only ever lost one Davis Cup rubber, against Spain, dropped the first set in the doubles to Horia Tecau and Marius Copil. The Romanians, actually, had some form, having come from two sets down to beat Marat Safin and Dmitry Tursunov in a tie in 2009. However, Berdych and Stepanek, are an entirely different proposition, as they eventually proved in winning 3–6 6–3 6–0 6–2.

After that, Czech Republic could afford to let Jan Hajek and Lukas Rosol enjoy themselves in the dead rubbers. Rosol is twenty-six and had never played Davis Cup before. Hajek, who lost both his singles rubbers against Kazakhstan, is twenty-eight. Even Berdych is twenty-six. Given that junior No. 1, Jiri Vesely, shoulders the weight of expectation for the future of Czech tennis, it's just as well for them that Stepanek has no immediate plans to retire.

"Tennis has gotten more physical, but as long as my body allows me to keep up with the other guys, I will keep playing," he said. "It takes hard work to do that, but so far I'm doing a good job."

Indeed he is. ●

Pictured clockwise from the top:

Radek Stepanek (CZE);

The crowd in Bucharest;

Adrian Ungur (ROU);

Czech fans

further in Cincinnati, as a qualifier, had he not run into Novak Djokovic in the third round.

However, the Czech Federation must have feared the worst when he retired in his second-round match against Juan Monaco at the US Open just a fortnight before the tie with an injury to his right, serving shoulder. Fortunately for them, he was able to recover in time to board the flight to the Romanian capital.

In fact, they were doubly fortunate because Victor Hanescu, the longtime Romanian No. 1, who had been struggling with his form since the French Open, pulled out to be replaced by Adrian Ungur, ranked No. 129 in the world. He was no match for Stepanek, and the Czechs breathed another sigh of relief as their man got them off on the right foot with a comfortable 6–3 6–2 6–0 victory.

Had Stepanek not been there to steady the ship, who knows what might have happened when leg cramps afflicted Czech No. 1, Tomas Berdych, for the first time in his career in the third set of his match against Victor Crivoi. The added pressure might have gotten to the world No. 7 in that second rubber. As it was, he was able to see his way out of difficulty against a player ranked more than two hundred places behind him to win 6–3 6–3 7–6(4).

"For the lower-ranked players it's a great experience to play against a top 10, top 20 guy," said the Romanian captain, Andrei Pavel, who was no mean player himself. "They can see that the difference is only

Shamil Tarpischev

There aren't many men in sport who preceded Sir Alex Ferguson into management and are still at the top of their game today, but Shamil Tarpischev is one. Moreover, he is captain of two teams—Russia's Davis Cup and Fed Cup sides—both of which he has steered to at least as much success as that enjoyed by Manchester United. But if tennis hadn't been regarded in the early 1970s in USSR as "a girly sport," we might never have heard of him, and as a result Russia might not be the powerhouse it is today.

Had tennis been an Olympic sport in those days, it's unlikely that the twenty-five-year-old Tarpischev would have been entrusted with the job of captaining the Davis Cup team. He might have instead ended up crossing swords with Ferguson in the Champions League because he was an avid student of football.

It was, in the words of Tarpischev himself, wrong to place someone of his age in charge of players "who were all older than me." How other countries must wish they had "blundered" similarly. Since then Russia, in the last decade, has won the Davis Cup on two occasions and the Fed Cup on four, narrowly missing out on a fifth title in Moscow in November 2011. Tarpischev, the inscrutable face of Russian tennis for

the past 37 years and 122 ties, has been the driving force behind that success—with a little help from his old friend, Boris Yeltsin, the former Soviet premier. In fact, Tarpischev, unselfishly, gives a lot of the credit to the late Yeltsin.

"When he showed up in public in shorts with a tennis racquet in his hand, he opened up the sport for the country at large," said Tarpischev, who will be sixty-four in March. "It was the start of the tennis boom. Before then it was regarded as a girly sport. Once he started backing tennis it got television coverage and sponsorship, and people started translating foreign books on tennis methodology. It became so much easier to work in tennis. It's hard to overestimate the importance of his involvement."

Likewise Tarpischev. The two men were both adept at talking people around to their way of thinking. They could almost have swapped roles. "In sport we talk about mobilizing one's nervous system," said Tarpischev, "which means doing your best in the worst situations, and Yeltsin had that sense. Of course, he was a recreational player, but in key moments he usually managed to win. It was the same in politics: when the going was tough he invariably made the right decisions."

One of Tarpischev's key moments, possibly even the turning point in his career, came during his second tie in charge in July 1974 against Czechoslovakia, when the fresh-faced captain managed to persuade Alexsandr Metreveli that all was not lost at 1–4 down in the fifth set of the fourth rubber against the former Wimbledon champion Jan Kodes. Metreveli went on to win and square the tie before Teimuraz Kakulia gave Russia victory in the deciding rubber. From then on the players began to listen to him.

"A captain has only to make a couple of mistakes and a player will stop believing in him," he said. "But at that time people forgave me my faults, because nobody really cared about tennis. Then, step-by-step, I piled up expertise and knowledge, and when I began to show some results there was no reason to fire me anymore."

It was twenty years before Russia under Tarpischev progressed beyond the first round in the World Group, but he didn't waste his time. He spent it laying the

foundations for Russia's future success with the formation of a scientific training center where a player's DNA and other criteria are examined to see whether he or she has the capability of becoming a champion.

As one of the first coaches to realize the importance of psychology in sport, he understood that the "egotistical" tennis player responded better to gentle persuasion than an iron fist. While others reminisce about Mikhail Youzhny's epic comeback against France's Paul-Henri Mathieu when winning the Davis Cup for Russia for the first time in 2002, Tarpischev prefers to recall the importance of convincing the elder statesman Yevgeny Kafelnikov that it made sense to replace him with the twenty-year-old Youzhny in that decisive final rubber.

"I needed to win the rubber and at the same time preserve the team's integrity—I succeeded in both endeavors," said Tarpischev.

Well though the Russian players have done on the grand slam stage, the rest of the world should just consider itself fortunate that because of lack of finance and insufficient training facilities, Russia has had to release its players to the outside world at the age of fourteen or, as Tarpischev put it, "evict" them. "That's my biggest pain," he said. "If we could prolong this preparation period at home until the age of eighteen, we would produce many more champions, and I would feel more serene about it." ●

UNDER A WATCHFUL EYE

Playing for your country inevitably means you will be under the media spotlight, and it's great to see players—with so many commitments these days—still find time to meet the fans.

Final 2-4 December

Spain defeated Argentina 3-1 Seville, Spain—Indoor Clay

The Final

Spain v Argentina

Only one thing in the world could have made victory in the climax to the 2011 Davis Cup by BNP Paribas any sweeter for Rafael Nadal, and that would have been to beat his nemesis, Novak Djokovic, in the decisive rubber. Unfortunately for some, the dream final between the defending champion, Serbia, and Spain—and with it the ultimate confrontation between the world No. 1 and No. 2—never materialized, because Djokovic's extraordinary season had finally run its course by the second week of September and because of Argentina's insatiable desire to be crowned champion.

Anyone who viewed a Spain-versus-Argentina final as a foregone conclusion was in for a surprise. Davis Cup never has been—and hopefully never will be—totally predictable, and the story of this final had all the twists and turns we have come to expect of this marvelous old competition. Who could have predicted that it would nearly go to a fifth and final rubber when Albert Costa's team led 2–0 at the end of the first day's play? Furthermore, who with any confidence could have predicted the winner of that fifth rubber had it come to pass between David Ferrer and, in all probability, the talismanic, enigmatic David Nalbandian?

As it was, a crowd of 24,852—one of the biggest in tennis history—witnessed a battle royale fit for King Juan Carlos of Spain in the decisive fourth rubber at the Olympic Stadium in Seville as Nadal and Juan Martin del Potro went toe to toe. Those who follow boxing as avidly as they do tennis might have been reminded of the epic 1985 middleweight title fight in which Marvelous Marvin Hagler, the then champion, took some quite unbelievable punishment from Thomas "the Hitman" Hearns only to come back and win by a stoppage. (The difference was that the Nadal–Del Potro "set-to" lasted about four hours longer.)

Nadal had arrived in the Andalusian city tired and seemingly spent after his premature exit a week earlier from the Barclays ATP World Tour Finals in London, where he had spoken—uncharacteristically—of losing passion for the game. With Spain's No. 2, David Ferrer, going deeper into the competition at the O2 Arena, there was a feeling that the balance of power in this Davis Cup final was shifting toward Argentina—or at least evening up a little. Meanwhile, the Argentines had spent three weeks at home practicing on the clay and resting with just one thought in mind: winning the Davis Cup for the first time in their history.

However, once back in the bosom of their native land, surrounded by their teammates, Nadal and Ferrer's competitive juices, inevitably, began flowing again. At the pre-match press conference following the draw at the Teatro Lope de Vega, a beautiful little Baroque-style theater, there was no more talk of tiredness. (Perhaps it was out of deference to the sixteenth-century Spanish playwright after whom the theater was named. With more than three thousand sonnets and eighteen hundred plays to his name, Lope de Vega was one of the most prolific authors in Western literature and presumably never complained about tiredness.)

Last time the two countries met, in the final of the 2008 competition at Mar del Plata, Argentina was beaten as much by internal strife as by the opposition. This time, under the even-handed management of Tito Vazquez, there was greater accord among the players even if some didn't see eye to eye. The pressure of favoritism was no longer upon them, and del Potro was now a better player, if a recovering one, than he was when he was injured in his opening rubber against Feliciano Lopez in 2008. But the really big difference this time was that they now had to contend with Nadal.

It is worth noting here that in the semifinal between Argentina and Serbia, which came hard on the heels of the delayed US Open final between Nadal and Djokovic, the Argentines had come to the conclusion that Djokovic would probably not be fit to give his best in the opening rubber. Consequently, they risked deploying both their big guns—del Potro and Nalbandian—on day one in order to get a flying start. It proved a smart move. Before the final they speculated similarly that Nadal's game might be lacking rhythm and that he might be tired after his exertions in London, but interestingly—and probably wisely—they chose not to do the same thing.

Had they thrown Nalbandian, their lucky mascot, into the fray on day one and he lost, as he might well have done, it would have meant that, quite apart from the psychological damage done to the team, he would almost certainly have been unavailable for the reverse singles, such is his fitness these days, and might not even have been able to turn out for the doubles. Instead Juan Monaco—a good friend of Nadal's—was offered as the sacrificial lamb in the opening rubber. No sacrificial lamb ever knew his fate better than Monaco: "I know him [Nadal] so well. Deep down, I knew that in the big moments he grows, he's a big player, and he gives his best."

It was hoped by the Argentine camp that Monaco, because of his fine end-of-season form, which had seen him reach the final of the Valencia tournament (in which he was beaten by Spain's first reserve Marcel Granollers) and the quarterfinals of the Paris Masters, might at least extend Nadal, exhaust him a little. Fat chance. But a twenty-four-place discrepancy in the rankings never looked wider. The 6–1 6–1 6–2 scoreline was misleading, since the match lasted two

hours, twenty-seven minutes, but only slightly.

Nadal revealed afterward, somewhat surprisingly, that he had felt a trifle nervous at the start of the third set, but it could be that he was just being generous to a friend. Of his nineteen consecutive singles victories in Davis Cup—fifteen of them without conceding a set—since losing to Czech Republic's Jiri Novak on his debut as a seventeen-year-old, this had to be one of his easiest. At least Monaco was in good company. Not since the Federal Republic of Germany's Boris Becker beat Mats Wilander, of Sweden, 6–2 6–0 6–2 in the title-clinching fourth rubber of 1989 had anyone won so few games in a final.

A week earlier, in losing to Jo-Wilfried Tsonga, of France, at the O2, Nadal had looked a spent force. Now he looked like a man who would be king again. Unlike the press, he wasn't getting carried away. In fact, no man could have his feet planted more firmly on the ground than Nadal, and he treated a question about whether he was human with the scorn it deserved. "Last week I was almost dead, and now people think that I'm not human," he said. "I don't think we can dramatize or exaggerate things either way. I wasn't there last week, and I am human this week."

Poor Monaco gave it his all—even hurling himself after a lost cause and receiving an injured wrist and bloody knee for his trouble. "I was suffering because I was thinking, 'Well, how can I get one point out of this guy?'" he said. "After that happened, it's difficult to

focus again; it's difficult to feel a winner again. Obviously I'm very sad, because nobody likes to lose this way, but I am also aware that in front of me I had one of the best tennis players in history."

One-zero to Spain was what everyone expected. One-one was what Argentina and all neutrals—not that there were too many of them among the partisan crowd—hoped for by the end of day one. Of course, it was a big ask of del Potro—as it would be of any player in the world—to beat the world No. 5 Ferrer on clay or anywhere else for that matter. In four meetings, surprisingly, they had never met on the orange stuff. But the big man is a force of nature, and Argentina was hopeful: in fact, their very dreams depended upon it. It was the first of the three rubbers they had targeted for overall victory, the other two being the doubles (hence the selection of doubles specialist Eduardo Schwank ahead of the more experienced Juan Ignacio Chela) and the fifth rubber.

The trumpet opening to the *Rocky* theme would have left del Potro in little doubt about the hard, long slog that awaited him if victory was to be yanked from the teeth of the terrier-like Ferrer. It wasn't the last time during this event that this choice of music would seem particularly apposite. The bigger they are, the harder they fall, the gritty little Spaniard surely thought to himself as he squared off against the six-foot, six-inch Argentine at the net.

In the opening games Ferrer frequently raced into a 40–0 lead before del Potro's massive forehand came into its own. But in the fourth game, on his own serve, the Argentine was unable to rescue himself, and on the second of three break points he was broken. His one chance of getting back on terms in the first set came and went with two break points in the seventh game. When Ferrer then broke del Potro to love to win the set, this anticipated marathon suddenly looked considerably more abbreviated, something more akin to a sprint. Del Potro, however, still had his eye on the long game.

Ferrer struggled to hold serve in the opening game of the second set, which was a little ominous for the Spanish, and then in the fifth game del Potro finally forced a break to the ecstatic delight of the Argentine fans. Although heavily outnumbered, they regularly outcheered and outsang the home fans, who to be

honest had a greater appreciation of tennis etiquette. The Argentine fans would have been equally at home supporting a team of Diego Maradona as Tito Vazquez. It was as much as the umpires Pascal Maria, of France, and Carlos Ramos, of Portugal, could do to keep a modicum of control throughout this tie.

Del Potro went on to consolidate the break before a couple of errant forehands allowed Ferrer to level at 4–4. Del Potro had a break point at 5–6 but lacked the courage to go to the net and finish the job. Eventually finding that courage, he took the set to a tiebreak which began positively for him thanks to a couple of overrules by umpire Ramos. Ferrer chose an inopportune moment to serve his first double fault of the match, thereby giving del Potro four set points.

Suddenly it was game on, but Argentine optimism was soon deflated when Ferrer broke in the opening game of the third set. Del Potro stayed with it though and broke back to level before taking a 5–3 lead on the Ferrer serve with some huge hitting. His biggest weapon remained in good shape as he held to take a two-sets-to-one lead. Against anyone else, a player would be entitled to start feeling a little confident, but against Ferrer it would be a mistake. The man never knows when he is beaten, and in the fourth game of the fourth set, del Potro's fourth double fault of the match saw him surrender his serve and the initiative, only for del Potro to immediately break back.

By now the match was under floodlights, and this semi-outdoor venue took on the ambience of an evening football cup tie. It was turning into a slugfest, which suited Ferrer down to the ground. Before we knew it he was level at two-sets-all, and one had the feeling del Potro may have missed his opportunity, although there had been so many swings in momentum no one could be too sure.

When Ferrer declined to run down a drop shot in the second game of the fifth set, the Argentines prayed that this was one Duracell bunny whose battery had run down. They should have known better. Two inside-out forehands from Ferrer gave del Potro a taste of his own medicine and had Nadal standing on his chair courtside roaring his teammate on to a 3–1 lead. In its twelve-year existence the stadium, which has been the cornerstone of two failed bids to stage the Olympics, rarely experienced such an atmosphere.

Pictured clockwise from top right: Eduardo Schwank (ARG) and David Nalbandian (ARG); The Spanish bench; Feliciano Lopez (ESP) and Fernando Verdasco (ESP); Argentina captain Tito Vazquez writes in the clay

Both the stadium and del Potro were rocking, but in different ways. Ferrer, who at twenty-nine was six-and-a-half years the elder, had finally broken the big man's spirit. Del Potro dropped serve again but pluckily clawed one back before finally succumbing 6–2 6–7(2) 3–6 6–4 6–3 in fourteen minutes shy of five hours. The Argentine was distraught, sobbing into his towel as he left the court with his head bowed, but he had played his part in a magnificent match and was magnanimous in his praise of Ferrer afterward. "All the points were very long and that's the way he likes it," said del Potro. "He has had a spectacular season, and nobody has given the victory as a gift to him. He's earned it."

Only one team in the 112-year history of the competition had come back from 0–2 down in the final to win, and that was Australia, also away, against the United States in 1939. Like Argentina, it too had lost the opening-day rubbers in three sets and five but had an outstanding doubles pair in John Bromwich and Adrian Quist to get them back into the tie. The Argentine duo of Nalbandian and Schwank was not a recognized pairing but had prepared well and was confident of beating Spain's pairing of Lopez and Fernando Verdasco, who had lost ten of their last eleven matches in all competitions.

The question was whether the Argentines still had the inclination or the desire necessary to win. It didn't take long to realize that they did. Their fanatical supporters expected nothing less. The Spaniards had lost badly to the French in their semifinal and were keen to make amends, but their old frailties soon resurfaced in the fifth game as Lopez, a natural serve-volleyer, dumped two volleys in the net on his way to dropping serve.

Playing in his first Davis Cup final, Schwank felt the pressure for the first time as he served for the set. A timely interception from Nalbandian manufactured a set point, which the Argentines took. Time and again Nalbandian's experience was key. Verdasco had

Spaniards were the more experienced pairing but no one would have guessed it. Nalbandian and Schwank, on the other hand, were playing together for the first time in Davis Cup.

The second set went away from Spain quickly after that, and it would take an enormous sea change for the home country to realize their aim of victory inside two days. They couldn't have started the third set worse as they lost four points in a row on the Lopez serve. The way Verdasco was bouncing around, clenching his fist, anyone would have thought Spain was up two sets instead of Argentina, but this fooled no one.

The Spanish crowd momentarily got behind their men when they forced two break points in the sixth game, but it didn't last, and in less than two hours Argentina was back in this tie courtesy of a 6–4 6–2 6–3 win. Now it was all up to del Potro. On the face of it, his chances of beating Nadal were not good. His opening-day match had been twice as long as Nadal's, and there were still issues surrounding his fitness as he clawed his way back up the rankings after a serious wrist operation that had caused him to miss two years of Davis Cup play.

While his forehand was still a weapon on clay, the ball came back too often for his liking, and he didn't move too well on the surface, unlike his opponent, of course, who might have been born with clay between his toes. Nor did the head-to-head record—6–3 in Nadal's favor—offer much encouragement. No doubt his captain would have reminded him of what happened in 2009, when even before del Potro had officially come of age he matured as a player, beating Nadal on three consecutive occasions. The last time was in straight sets at the US Open, when del Potro won his first and only grand slam title before injury cruelly interrupted his career. It made Nadal arguably more respectful of him than any player he had previously faced. Indeed del Potro threatened to dominate him—and the rest of the world's top players—in much the same way that Djokvoic would two years later.

Before del Potro went out to face Nadal, Vazquez scrawled the words "No Fear" in the dust in front of his player's chair. And fearless he was. Fans of either persuasion could not believe their eyes as the

Pictured opposite:

Rafael Nadal (ESP)

Pictured above:

Rafael Nadal (ESP) and Juan Martin del Potro (ARG); The Spanish team

chosen to stay back on his serve, which cost him in the opening game of the second set as the Spanish were out-rallied from the baseline.

It wasn't long before the Spaniards, who were rapidly losing confidence, were a double break down. It was debatable which of them was playing worse. The

Argentine, recovering from an ignominious start, proceeded to batter Nadal from pillar to net post. It was hard to recall ever seeing Nadal so outclassed, so outmuscled. It was little wonder that afterward Nadal predicted his opponent would be "unstoppable" in 2012 and a contender for the No. 1 ranking, injury permitting.

At 2–1 up the Argentine fans were beside themselves with joy, and twice their celebrations interrupted Nadal as he shaped to serve. The Spaniard could be excused for inquiring just who was supposed to be playing at home. It wasn't until del Potro raised his arms imploringly that they quietened down. But he had no intention of quelling the storm in his own game. With admittedly some help from his opponent, he went on to break Nadal four times in an unbroken run of seven games, which included coming back from 0–40 down on his own serve to take the set.

It was then, at 40–0 and a break up in the second set, that the veil of invincibility began to slip from the Argentine's facade. Most players would have accepted the inevitable after the first set, but in this most gladiatorial of sports, Nadal has few equals. It seems almost unfair that the two gutsiest players in the world are both Spanish. Somehow Nadal managed to win five points on the trot to break del Potro. The distinct impression that we had reached a turning point was underlined when, in game five, Nadal held to love for the first time. And when he reeled off five consecutive service games to love, taking him to one-set-all and a 3–0 lead in the third, we knew the momentum was truly with the man dressed in red and yellow.

Without wishing to devalue Nadal's achievement, del Potro did look as if Friday's exertions had taken their toll on him. Not even five successive net cords in the Argentine's favor could convince him that the gods were on his side. And when Nadal raced through the third set and del Potro dropped the opening service game of the fourth, most Argentines were ready to pack their bags. It was a moot point whether Nalbandian had left courtside to do just that or prepare for a possible fifth rubber.

For whatever reason, at love-two down, the Argentine fans broke into song—and it wasn't "Don't Cry for Me Argentina." Whether the extended delay was unsettling for Nadal or recuperative for del Potro no one will know, but when play resumed the Argentine came back strongly to hold serve to love, which he hadn't done for an eternity—or so it seemed. Nadal just recalled playing some "very ugly drives"

Pictured clockwise from top right: The victorious Spanish team; Spain captain Albert Costa; King Juan Carlos, Spain captain Albert Costa, Rafael Nadal (ESP) and David Ferrer (ESP); Rafael Nadal (ESP) and David Ferrer (ESP)

into the net. In the next game del Potro broke back, raising his fist in salutation toward the steep bank of adoring Argentine fans at one end of the court. It seemed to galvanize him, and suddenly we hoped that Nalbandian was indeed practicing on the outside court rather than laying his clothes out for packing.

Three consecutive breaks of serve left the audience no more enlightened before del Potro broke again to find himself serving to take the match into a fifth set and possibly a fifth rubber. But the stubborn Nadal of course broke straight back. Then it was Nadal's turn to serve for the trophy only for del Potro to break back. The two men were running abreast for the line in true Olympic stadium fashion when in the last few steps—the fourth-set tiebreaker—del Potro fatally stumbled, his race run, and lost 1–6 6–4 6–1 7–6(0). Nadal had played arguably his best and worst sets of the year all in one match.

Vazquez turned to his words in the dust, scraped them away, and wrote "The End," which it may be for him but hopefully not for this Argentine team, which still has the potential to win the trophy in the next year or two. Nadal's first thoughts were for the losers and

he quickly prised himself free of the clutches of his delirious teammates to commiserate with del Potro at the net before embracing each and every member of the Argentine team. Later, King Juan Carlos himself was no less effusive with each of the Spanish players.

Of all Spain's five title successes since 2000, this was arguably the most enjoyable and the most emotional, eclipsing even Nadal's first Davis Cup triumph, at the age of eighteen, in this same stadium against the United States in 2004 when his good friend and mentor Carlos Moya—a possible successor to Costa as captain—was the main man. With time Nadal has learned to savor his victories.

Smiling more broadly than he had all year, he commented, "When you're young, everything is new, and you don't have the capacity to truly enjoy and comprehend the difficulty of the situation. But after you've been here for many years, you understand there are ups and downs and that you need to fight to be there all the time."

Despite Nadal's disappointments in tournament play, 2011—largely thanks to the Davis Cup—turned out to be a very good year for him. ●

Player of the Year: David Ferrer

Born April 2 1982 in Javea, Spain
Turned professional 2000

The incurable romantics among many of the impartial observers at the Davis Cup Final in Seville liked to think that if the tie had gone to a fifth rubber, David Nalbandian would have put aside all his fitness issues, stepped up to the plate, and won the trophy for the first time for Argentina, thereby bringing to an end ten years of personal underachievement. Nice story, and possibly a deserving one––particularly if you happened to be from Argentina––but it overlooked one crucial factor: David Ferrer.

Of course, being overlooked, you might say, is the story of the Spanish No. 2's life. Whenever the business end of tournaments like grand slams is discussed, you can rest assure that one name will be regularly missing from the list of usual suspects. This is partly because the world No. 5 has never made a grand slam final but also because he doesn't have a game that hits you straight between the eyes. He doesn't have a 140mph serve, a withering forehand or backhand, a thumping volley, or blistering speed. And at five feet, nine inches, he doesn't even cut an imposing figure: he just does everything very well, albeit from the baseline, and he does it consistently and relentlessly.

Andy Roddick is never short of something to say, even in his darkest moments, and when he lost their Davis Cup quarterfinal rubber in straight sets in July, he summed up perfectly how many top players on the wrong end of a beating from Ferrer feel: "I have too much respect for Ferrer to act like I'm stunned."

The Argentine No. 1, Juan Martin del Potro, is one of those "usual suspects" who would second those sentiments, as probably would Nalbandian. In the final del Potro led Ferrer two sets to one in the second rubber but would have known that the next set would be the hardest because "defeat" is a word that sticks in Ferrer's craw. The big man ended up losing a memorable match in five sets, but it may have been some consolation to him to know that Ferrer described it as "maybe the best match of my career."

"It is not only my job to fight, but my honor as well," Ferrer said. "And I must do it till that last point. The sport of tennis is one of respect, and I feel that if I respect tennis and my fellow players, then I have done my duty."

The Valenciano more than did his duty, both for himself and his country, in 2011. He made himself available for every tie and was a key figure in every round apart from the first, against Belgium, when he had to pull out at the last moment with a shoulder injury. Against the United States in Austin, Texas, his straight sets victory over Roddick in the second rubber was crushing for the home team. He then he went out and clinched the tie in a desperately close four-setter against the American No. 1, Mardy Fish.

Modest to a fault, he deserved his moment in the spotlight then because, with the likes of Rafael Nadal around, it doesn't happen very often. In the semifinal against France, Nadal rightly took the plaudits for traveling straight after a demoralizing defeat to Novak Djokovic in New York to Cordoba, where he won both his rubbers, on a different surface, in straight sets. But Ferrer was no less impressive in his defeat of Gilles Simon.

Ever the bridesmaid, and yet no No. 2 was ever less grudging in his praise of a No. 1. Although Spain won the Davis Cup in 2008 without Nadal, Ferrer has always stressed that they would never have reached the final without Nadal's contribution in the earlier rounds, and he credits him for raising the bar and lifting his fellow countrymen into the upper echelons of the game.

Ferrer is a confident performer today, someone a team like Spain can bank on in a fifth rubber, but this wasn't always the case. He had something of an inferiority complex in his early days, which came from practicing regularly with the likes of Marat Safin and Juan Carlos Ferrero. His elder brother, Javier, who was a national champion at under-12, failed to make the transition to the senior ranks, and for a while it looked as if young David would struggle, too, because according to Javier Piles, his coach, he was not a great trainer.

Now however the twenty-nine-year-old never stops striving to be better, and the books he reads on tour invariably have something to do with self-improvement. "He does not want praise," said Piles. "He wants information on how to get better."

Though he may be in danger of inheriting from Nalbandian the unwanted epithet of "the greatest player of his generation never to win a grand slam," with such dedication, Ferrer may yet win a major one day to put alongside the three Davis Cup titles he holds. ●

ALL THE FUN OF THE FINAL

Both teams entered the Davis Cup by BNP Paribas final intent on lifting the historic trophy, but nothing could prevent the players from enjoying every moment of competing for their country on the biggest stage.

119

WORLD GROUP

First round 4-6 March
Serbia defeated India 4-1, Novi Sad, Serbia, Hard (I): Viktor Troicki (SRB) d. Rohan Bopanna (IND) 63 63 57 36 63; Somdev Devvarman (IND) d. Janko Tipsarevic (SRB) 75 75 76(3); Ilija Bozoljac/Nenad Zimonjic (SRB) d. Rohan Bopanna/Somdev Devvarman (IND) 46 63 64 76(10); Viktor Troicki (SRB) d. Somdev Devvarman (IND) 64 62 75; Janko Tipsarevic (SRB) d. Karan Rastogi (IND) 60 61.

Sweden defeated Russia 3-2, Boras, Sweden, Hard (I): Robin Soderling (SWE) d. Igor Andreev (RUS) 63 63 61; Joachim Johansson (SWE) d. Teymuraz Gabashvili (RUS) 63 76(4) 64; Simon Aspelin/Robert Lindstedt (SWE) d. Igor Kunitsyn/Dmitry Tursunov (RUS) 64 67(6) 76(6) 62; Dmitry Tursunov (RUS) d. Simon Aspelin (SWE) 75 62; Igor Andreev (RUS) d. Joachim Johansson (SWE) 76(8) 64.

Kazakhstan defeated Czech Republic 3-2, Ostrava, Czech Republic, Hard (I): Andrey Golubev (KAZ) d. Jan Hajek (CZE) 76(4) 67(3) 16 76(4) 63; Tomas Berdych (CZE) d. Mikhail Kukushkin (KAZ) 76(5) 62 63; Tomas Berdych/Lukas Dlouhy (CZE) d. Evgeny Korolev/Yuriy Schukin (KAZ) 64 64 76(4); Andrey Golubev (KAZ) d. Tomas Berdych (CZE) 75 57 64 62; Mikhail Kukushkin (KAZ) d. Jan Hajek (CZE) 64 67(4) 76(8) 60.

Argentina defeated Romania 4-1, Buenos Aires, Argentina, Clay (O): David Nalbandian (ARG) d. Adrian Ungur (ROU) 63 62 57 64; Juan Monaco (ARG) d. Victor Hanescu (ROU) 76(5) 16 61 61; Juan Ignacio Chela/Eduardo Schwank (ARG) d. Victor Hanescu/Horia Tecau (ROU) 62 76(8) 61; Eduardo Schwank (ARG) d. Victor Crivoi (ROU) 76(3) 62; Adrian Ungur (ROU) d. Juan Monaco (ARG) 64 26 63.

USA defeated Chile 4-1, Santiago, Chile, Clay (O): Andy Roddick (USA) d. Nicolas Massu (CHI) 62 46 63 64; Paul Capdeville (CHI) d. John Isner (USA) 67(5) 67(2) 76(3) 76(5) 64; Bob Bryan/Mike Bryan (USA) d. Jorge Aguilar/Nicolas Massu (CHI) 63 63 76(4); Andy Roddick (USA) d. Paul Capdeville (CHI) 36 76(2) 63 63; John Isner (USA) d. Guillermo Rivera-Aranguiz (CHI) 63 67(4) 75.

Spain defeated Belgium 4-1, Charleroi, Belgium, Hard (I): Fernando Verdasco (ESP) d. Xavier Malisse (BEL) 64 63 61; Rafael Nadal (ESP) d. Ruben Bemelmans (BEL) 62 64 62; Feliciano Lopez/Fernando Verdasco (ESP) d. Steve Darcis/Olivier Rochus (BEL) 76(0) 64 63; Rafael Nadal (ESP) d. Olivier Rochus (BEL) 64 62; Steve Darcis (BEL) d. Feliciano Lopez (ESP) 67(4) 76(6) 76(3).

Germany defeated Croatia 3-2, Zagreb, Croatia, Hard (I): Marin Cilic (CRO) d. Florian Mayer (GER) 46 60 46 63 61; Philipp Kohlschreiber (GER) d. Ivan Dodig (CRO) 64 36 46 76(6) 64; Christopher Kas/Philipp Petzschner (GER) d. Ivan Dodig/Ivo Karlovic (CRO) 63 36 57 63 64; Marin Cilic (CRO) d. Philipp Kohlschreiber (GER) 62 63 76(6); Philipp Petzschner (GER) d. Ivo Karlovic (CRO) 64 76(3) 76(5).

France defeated Austria 3-2, Vienna, Austria, Clay (I): Jeremy Chardy (FRA) d. Jurgen Melzer (AUT) 75 64 75; Gilles Simon (FRA) d. Stefan Koubek (AUT) 60 62 63; Oliver Marach/Jurgen Melzer (AUT) d. Julien Benneteau/Michael Llodra (FRA) 64 36 63 64; Jurgen Melzer (AUT) d. Gilles Simon (FRA) 76(7) 36 16 64 60; Jeremy Chardy (FRA) d. Martin Fischer (AUT) 26 76(4) 63 63.

Quarterfinals 8-10 July
Argentina defeated Kazakhstan 5-0, Buenos Aires, Argentina, Clay (O): Juan Monaco (ARG) d. Andrey Golubev (KAZ) 63 60 64; Juan Martin del Potro (ARG) d. Mikhail Kukushkin (KAZ) 62 61 62; Juan Ignacio Chela/Eduardo Schwank (ARG) d. Evgeny Korolev/Yuriy Schukin (KAZ) 63 62 75; Juan Ignacio Chela (ARG) d. Evgeny Korolev (KAZ) 26 62 60; Juan Monaco (ARG) d. Mikhail Kukushkin (KAZ) 64 61.

Serbia defeated Sweden 4-1, Halmstad, Sweden, Hard (I): Viktor Troicki (SRB) d. Michael Ryderstedt (SWE) 63 61 67(6) 75; Janko Tipsarevic (SRB) d. Ervin Eleskovic (SWE) 62 10 ret; Simon Aspelin/Robert Lindstedt (SWE) d. Novak Djokovic/Nenad Zimonjic (SRB) 64 76(5) 75; Janko Tipsarevic (SRB) d. Michael Ryderstedt (SWE) 62 75 63; Viktor Troicki (SRB) d. Robert Lindstedt (SWE) 36 64 ret.

Spain defeated USA 3-1, Austin, TX, USA, Hard (I): Feliciano Lopez (ESP) d. Mardy Fish (USA) 64 36 63 67(2) 86; David Ferrer (ESP) d. Andy Roddick (USA) 76(9) 75 63; Bob Bryan/Mike Bryan (USA) d. Marcel Granollers/Fernando Verdasco (ESP) 67(3) 64 64 64; David Ferrer (ESP) d. Mardy Fish (USA) 75 76(3) 57 76(5).

France defeated Germany 4-1, Stuttgart, Germany, Clay (O): Richard Gasquet (FRA) d. Florian Mayer (GER) 46 46 75 63 63; Gael Monfils (FRA) d. Philipp Kohlschreiber (GER) 76(3) 76(5) 64; Michael Llodra/Jo-Wilfried Tsonga (FRA) d. Christopher Kas/Philipp Petzschner (GER) 76(4) 64 64; Philipp Petzschner (GER) d. Michael Llodra (FRA) 63 64; Jo-Wilfried Tsonga (FRA) d. Philipp Kohlschreiber (GER) 76(3) 76(5).

Semifinals 16-18 September
Argentina defeated Serbia 3-2, Belgrade, Serbia, Hard (I): David Nalbandian (ARG) d. Viktor Troicki (SRB) 64 46 62 63; Juan Martin del Potro (ARG) d. Janko Tipsarevic (SRB) 75 63 64; Viktor Troicki/Nenad Zimonjic (SRB) d. Juan Ignacio Chela/Juan Monaco (ARG) 76(4) 64 62; Juan Martin del Potro (ARG) d. Novak Djokovic (SRB) 76(5) 30 ret.; Janko Tipsarevic (SRB) d. Juan Monaco (ARG) 62 ret.

Spain defeated France 4-1, Cordoba, Spain, Clay (O): Rafael Nadal (ESP) d. Richard Gasquet (FRA) 63 60 61; David Ferrer (ESP) d. Gilles Simon (FRA) 61 64 61; Michael Llodra/Jo-Wilfried Tsonga (FRA) d. Feliciano Lopez/Fernando Verdasco (ESP) 61 62 60; Rafael Nadal (ESP) d. Jo-Wilfried Tsonga (FRA) 60 62 64; Fernando Verdasco (ESP) d. Richard Gasquet (FRA) 62 61.

Final 2-4 December
Spain defeated Argentina 3-1, Seville, Spain, Clay (I): Rafael Nadal (ESP) d. Juan Monaco (ARG) 61 61 62; David Ferrer (ESP) d. Juan Martin del Potro (ARG) 62 67(2) 36 64 63; David Nalbandian/Eduardo Schwank (ARG) d. Feliciano Lopez/Fernando Verdasco (ESP) 64 62 63; Rafael Nadal (ESP) d. Juan Martin del Potro (ARG) 16 64 61 76(0).

World Group play-offs 16-18 September
Czech Republic defeated Romania 5-0, Bucharest, Romania, Clay (O): Radek Stepanek (CZE) d. Adrian Ungur (ROU) 63 62 60; Tomas Berdych (CZE) d. Victor Crivoi (ROU) 63 63 76(4); Tomas Berdych/Radek Stepanek (CZE) d. Marius Copil/Horia Tecau (ROU) 36 63 60 62; Lukas Rosol (CZE) d. Marius Copil (ROU) 64 76(2); Jan Hajek (CZE) d. Victor Crivoi (ROU) 61 64.

Russia defeated Brazil 3-2, Kazan, Russia, Hard (I): Mikhail Youzhny (RUS) d. Ricardo Mello (BRA) 60 62 61; Thomaz Bellucci (BRA) d. Igor Andreev (RUS) 64 63 63; Marcelo Melo/Bruno Soares (BRA) d. Igor Kunitsyn/Dmitry Tursunov (RUS) 64 75 62; Mikhail Youzhny (RUS) d. Thomaz Bellucci (BRA) 26 63 57 64 1412; Dmitry Tursunov (RUS) d. Ricardo Mello (BRA) 61 76(5) 26 63.

Canada defeated Israel 3-2, Ramat Hasharon, Israel, Hard (O): Vasek Pospisil (CAN) d. Dudi Sela (ISR) 76(4) 67(6) 61 67(2) 63; Amir Weintraub (ISR) d. Milos Raonic (CAN) 57 75 63 61; Daniel Nestor/Vasek Pospisil (CAN) d. Jonathan Erlich/Andy Ram (ISR) 46 63 64 64; Dudi Sela (ISR) d. Peter Polansky (CAN) 63 63 63; Vasek Pospisil (CAN) d. Amir Weintraub (ISR) 62 76(3) 64.

Croatia defeated South Africa 4-1, Potchefstroom, South Africa, Hard (O): Kevin Anderson (RSA) d. Ivan Dodig (CRO) 63 63 64 76(5); Marin Cilic (CRO) d. Izak van der Merwe (RSA) 60 60 ret.; Marin Cilic/Ivan Dodig (CRO) d. Rik de Voest/Raven Klaasen (RSA) 62 64 36 61; Marin Cilic (CRO) d. Rik de Voest (RSA) 64 62 64; Nikola Mektic (CRO) d. Raven Klaasen (RSA) 76(2) 61.

Italy defeated Chile 4-1, Santiago, Chile, Hard (O): Potito Starace (ITA) d. Paul Capdeville (CHI) 63 63 26 76(5); Fabio Fognini (ITA) d. Fernando Gonzalez (CHI) 62 46 21 ret.; Simone Bolelli/Fabio Fognini (ITA) d. Jorge Aguilar/Nicolas Massu (CHI) 64 64 64; Paul Capdeville (CHI) d. Simone Bolelli (ITA) 76(3) 62; Daniele Bracciali (ITA) d. Nicolas Massu (CHI) 43 ret.

Japan defeated India 4-1, Tokyo, Japan, Hard (O): Yuichi Sugita (JPN) d. Somdev Devvarman (IND) 63 64 75; Kei Nishikori (JPN) d. Rohan Bopanna (IND) 63 62 62; Mahesh Bhupathi/Rohan Bopanna (IND) d. Tatsuma Ito/Yuichi Sugita (JPN) 75 36 63 76(4); Kei Nishikori (JPN) d. Vishnu Vardhan (IND) 75 63 63; Go Soeda (JPN) d. Rohan Bopanna (IND) 45 ret.

Austria defeated Belgium 4-1, Antwerp, Belgium, Hard (I): Andreas Haider-Maurer (AUT) d. Xavier Malisse (BEL) 64 64 75; Steve Darcis (BEL) d. Jurgen Melzer (AUT) 76(3) 67(4) 64 63; Oliver Marach/Alexander Peya (AUT) d. Steve Darcis/Olivier Rochus (BEL) 46 63 64 64; Jurgen Melzer (AUT) d. Olivier Rochus (BEL) 64 64 63; Alexander Peya (AUT) d. Ruben Bemelmans (BEL) 64 63.

Switzerland defeated Australia 3-2, Sydney, Australia, Grass (O): Bernard Tomic (AUS) d. Stanislas Wawrinka (SUI) 46 64 63 63; Roger Federer (SUI) d. Lleyton Hewitt (AUS) 57 76(5) 62 63; Chris Guccione/Lleyton Hewitt (AUS) d. Roger Federer/Stanislas Wawrinka (SUI) 26 64 62 76(5); Roger Federer (SUI) d. Bernard Tomic (AUS) 62 75 36 63; Stanislas Wawrinka (SUI) d. Lleyton Hewitt (AUS) 46 64 67(7) 64 63.

GROUP I

Americas Zone
First round 4-6 March
Canada defeated Mexico 4-1, Estado de Mexico, Mexico, Clay (O): Daniel Garza (MEX) d. Frank Dancevic (CAN) 26 46 62 63 64; Milos Raonic (CAN) d. Manuel Sanchez (MEX) 62 62 61; Vasek Pospisil/Milos Raonic (CAN) d. Luis Diaz-Barriga/Miguel-Angel Reyes-Varela (MEX) 46 63 64 64; Milos Raonic (CAN) d. Daniel Garza (MEX) 75 63 62; Peter Polansky (CAN) d. Manuel Sanchez (MEX) 64 61.

Uruguay defeated Colombia 4-1, Montevideo, Uruguay, Clay (O): Pablo Cuevas (URU) d. Alejandro Falla (COL) 26 61 62 64; Santiago Giraldo (COL) d. Martin Cuevas (URU) 62 60 62; Pablo Cuevas/Marcel Felder (URU) d. Juan-Sebastian Cabal/Robert Farah (COL) 16 76(6) 16 76(5) 62; Pablo Cuevas (URU) d. Santiago Giraldo (COL) 62 63 64; Marcel Felder (URU) d. Alejandro Falla (COL) 76(3) 67(2) 63.

Second round 8-10 July
Canada defeated Ecuador 3-2, Guayaquil, Ecuador, Clay (O): Ivan Endara (ECU) d. Vasek Pospisil (CAN) 63 64 67(6) 63; Julio-Cesar Campozano (ECU) d. Philip Bester (CAN) 76(4) 67(4) 75 62; Daniel Nestor/Vasek Pospisil (CAN) d. Emilio Gomez/Roberto Quiroz (ECU) 76(4) 64 75; Vasek Pospisil (CAN) d. Julio-Cesar Campozano (ECU) 63 64 75; Philip Bester (CAN) d. Ivan Endara (ECU) 62 76(3) 64.

Brazil defeated Uruguay 5-0, Montevideo, Uruguay, Clay (O): Rogerio Dutra Silva (BRA) d. Marcel Felder (URU) 62 62 63; Thomaz Bellucci (BRA) d. Martin Cuevas (URU) 61 64 75; Thomaz Bellucci/Bruno Soares (BRA) d. Martin Cuevas/Marcel Felder (URU) 64 63 63; Bruno Soares (BRA) d. Ariel Behar (URU) 62 62; Rogerio Dutra Silva (BRA) d. Martin Cuevas (URU) 63 76(4).

Brazil and Canada advanced to the World Group play-offs on 16-18 September 2011.

First round relegation play-off 16-18 September
Ecuador defeated Mexico 3-2, Guayaquil, Ecuador, Clay (O): Julio-Cesar Campozano (ECU) d. Miguel Gallardo-Valles (MEX) 62 46 63 62; Ivan Endara (ECU) d. Daniel Garza (MEX) 67(4) 76(0) 64 26 64; Daniel Garza/Santiago Gonzalez (MEX) d. Julio-Cesar Campozano/Roberto Quiroz (ECU) 62 67(6) 63 64; Julio-Cesar Campozano (ECU) d. Daniel Garza (MEX) 60 63 61; Miguel Gallardo-Valles (MEX) d. Juan-Sebastian Vivanco (ECU) 63 63.

Second round relegation play-off 28-30 October
Colombia defeated Mexico 5-0, Mexico City, Mexico, Clay (O): Santiago Giraldo (COL) d. Santiago Gonzalez (MEX) 64 76(5) 62; Alejandro Falla (COL) d. Cesar Ramirez (MEX) 16 61 61 63; Juan-Sebastian Cabal/Robert Farah (COL) d. Santiago Gonzalez/Cesar Ramirez (MEX) 76(7) 46 63 64; Robert Farah (COL) d. Luis Diaz-Barriga (MEX) 62 63. Juan-Sebastian Cabal (COL) d. Marco Aurelio Nunez (MEX) 61 62.

Mexico relegated to Americas Zone Group II in 2012.

Asia/Oceania Zone
First round 4-6 March
China, P.R. defeated Chinese Taipei 3-2, Shanghai, China, P.R., Hard (I): Mao-Xin Gong (CHN) d. Tsung-Hua Yang (TPE) 57 61 76(5) 46 86; Di Wu (CHN) d. Yen-Hsun Lu (TPE) 64 36 36 75 97; Yen-Hsun Lu/Tsung-Hua Yang (TPE) d. Mao-Xin Gong/Zhe Li (CHN) 75 64 67(3) 76(4); Yen-Hsun Lu (TPE) d. Mao-Xin Gong (CHN) 61 62 62; Di Wu (CHN) d. Tsung-Hua Yang (TPE) 63 62 26 60.

Japan defeated Philippines 3-1, Lapu-Lapu City, Philippines, Clay (O): Tatsuma Ito (JPN) d. Cecil Mamiit (PHI) 64 67(5) 63 67(3) 97; Go Soeda (JPN) d. Johnny Arcilla (PHI) 63 63 63; Treat Huey/Cecil Mamiit (PHI) d. Hiroki Kondo/Takao Suzuki (JPN) 61 76(5) 62; Go Soeda (JPN) d. Cecil Mamiit (PHI) 76(5) 62 36 63.

Uzbekistan defeated New Zealand 3-2, Namangan, Uzbekistan, Clay (I): Farrukh Dustov (UZB) d. Artem Sitak (NZL) 60 63 61; Denis Istomin (UZB) d. Jose Statham (NZL) 62 63 63; Farrukh Dustov/Denis Istomin (UZB) d. Marcus Daniell/Michael Venus (NZL) 76(5) 63 64; Artem Sitak (NZL) d. Murad Inoyatov (UZB) 61 67(2) 63; Michael Venus (NZL) d. Vaja Uzakov (UZB) 63 60.

Second round 8-10 July
Australia defeated China, P.R. 3-1, Beijing, China, P.R., Hard (I): Di Wu (CHN) d. Marinko Matosevic (AUS) 46 63 36 64 64; Bernard Tomic (AUS) d. Ze Zhang (CHN) 63 57 64 64; Chris Guccione/Lleyton Hewitt (AUS) d. Mao-Xin Gong/Zhe Li (CHN) 64 64 64; Lleyton Hewitt (AUS) d. Ze Zhang (CHN) 62 61 46 76(2).

Japan defeated Uzbekistan 4-1, Kobe, Japan, Hard (I): Denis Istomin (UZB) d. Tatsuma Ito (JPN) 64 64 64; Kei Nishikori (JPN) d. Farrukh Dustov (UZB) 67(2) 63 61 ret.; Kei Nishikori/Go Soeda (JPN) d. Murad Inoyatov/Denis Istomin (UZB) 75 76(5) 75; Kei Nishikori (JPN) d. Denis Istomin (UZB) 67(5) 75 64 63; Go Soeda (JPN) d. Sarvar Ikramov (UZB) 75 60.

Australia and Japan advanced to the World Group play-offs on 16-18 September 2011.

First round relegation play-off 8-10 July
New Zealand defeated Philippines 5-0, Hawera, New Zealand, Hard (I): Jose Statham (NZL) d. Ruben Gonzales (PHI) 64 64 64; Michael Venus (NZL) d. Cecil Mamiit (PHI) 67(6) 76(4) 63 46 63; Marcus Daniell/Artem Sitak (NZL) d. Ruben Gonzales/Cecil Mamiit (PHI) 76(0) 63 62; Marcus Daniell (NZL) d. Jeson Patrombon (PHI) 46 63 63; Artem Sitak (NZL) d. Cecil Mamiit (PHI) 64 75.

Second round relegation play-off 16-18 September
Chinese Taipei defeated Philippines 3-2, Lapu-Lapu, Philippines, Clay (O): Ti Chen (TPE) d. Cecil Mamiit (PHI) 67(2) 62 76(6) 63; Treat Huey (PHI) d. Jimmy Wang (TPE) 64 64 63; Hsin-Han Lee/Chu-Huan Yi (TPE) d. Treat Huey/Cecil Mamiit (PHI) 36 64 26 63 86; Ti Chen (TPE) d. Treat Huey (PHI) 63 76(2) 62; Jeson Patrombon (PHI) d. Jimmy Wang (TPE) 16 64 63.

Philippines relegated to Asia/Oceania Zone Group II in 2012.

Europe/Africa Zone
First round 4-6 March
Slovenia defeated Finland 3-2, Ljubljana , Slovenia, Clay (I): Jarkko Nieminen (FIN) d. Grega Zemlja (SLO) 36 63 64 63; Blaz Kavcic (SLO) d. Harri Heliovaara (FIN) 46 62 63 64; Luka Gregorc/Grega Zemlja (SLO) d. Harri Heliovaara/Jarkko Nieminen (FIN) 67(5) 64 64 75; Jarkko Nieminen (FIN) d. Blaz Kavcic (SLO) 63 64 46 64; Grega Zemlja (SLO) d. Micke Kontinen (FIN) 26 63 63 63.

Netherlands defeated Ukraine 3-2, Kharkiv, Ukraine, Hard (I): Sergiy Stakhovsky (UKR) d. Robin Haase (NED) 61 64 67(2) 46 62; Thiemo de Bakker (NED) d. Illya Marchenko (UKR) 76(3) 76(6) 64; Thiemo de Bakker/Robin Haase (NED) d. Sergei Bubka/Sergiy Stakhovsky (UKR) 76(6) 67(5) 64 76(9); Sergiy Stakhovsky (UKR) d. Jesse Huta Galung (NED) 61 64 36 67(4) 64; Robin Haase (NED) d. Illya Marchenko (UKR) 67(0) 16 76(5) 64 62.

Portugal defeated Slovak Republic 4-1, Cruz Quebrada, Portugal, Clay (O): Frederico Gil (POR) d. Lukas Lacko (SVK) 62 62 61; Rui Machado (POR) d. Martin Klizan (SVK) 64 64 16 26 64; Michal Mertinak/Filip Polasek (SVK) d. Frederico Gil/Leonardo Tavares (POR) 63 64 16 61; Rui Machado (POR) d. Lukas Lacko (SVK) 64 36 64 60; Joao Sousa (POR) d. Martin Klizan (SVK) 62 41 ret.

Second round 4-6 March
Israel defeated Poland 3-2, Ramat Hasharon, Israel, Hard (O): Dudi Sela (ISR) d. Marcin Gawron (POL) 61 63 64; Amir Weintraub (ISR) d. Jerzy Janowicz (POL) 46 62 62 67(4) 63; Jonathan Erlich/Andy Ram (ISR) d. Mariusz Fyrstenberg/Marcin Matkowski (POL) 46 64 63 61; Jerzy Janowicz (POL) d. Dudi Sela (ISR) 76(5) 64; Marcin Gawron (POL) d. Amir Weintraub (ISR) w/o.

Italy defeated Slovenia 5-0, Arzachena, Italy, Clay (O): Fabio Fognini (ITA) d. Grega Zemlja (SLO) 16 64 64 64; Potito Starace (ITA) d. Blaz Kavcic (SLO) 36 63 62 64; Daniele Bracciali/Potito Starace (ITA) d. Blaz Kavcic/Grega Zemlja (SLO) 76(3) 76(4) 62; Fabio Fognini (ITA) d. Aljaz Bedene (SLO) 62 22 ret.; Simone Bolelli (ITA) d. Grega Zemlja (SLO) 75 63.

South Africa defeated Netherlands 3-1, Potchefstroom, South Africa, Hard (O): Robin Haase (NED) d. Rik de Voest (RSA) 67(5) 63 60 64; Kevin Anderson (RSA) d. Thomas Schoorel (NED) 67(5) 64 76(4) 61; Kevin Anderson/Rik de Voest (RSA) d. Robin Haase/Jesse Huta Galung (NED) 67(4) 62 64 64; Kevin Anderson (RSA) d. Robin Haase (NED) 63 36 62 62.

Switzerland defeated Portugal 5-0, Bern, Switzerland, Hard (I): Stanislas Wawrinka (SUI) d. Frederico Gil (POR) 75 63 64; Roger Federer (SUI) d. Rui Machado (POR) 57 63 64 62; Roger Federer/Stanislas Wawrinka (SUI) d. Frederico Gil/Leonardo Tavares (POR) 63 64 64; Marco Chiudinelli (SUI) d. Joao Sousa (POR) 63 64; Stanislas Wawrinka (SUI) d. Leonardo Tavares (POR) 76(1) 60.

Israel, Italy, South Africa and Switzerland advanced to the World Group play-offs on 16-18 September 2011.

Relegation play-off 16-18 September
Finland defeated Poland 3-2, Espoo, Finland, Hard (I): Henri Kontinen (FIN) d. Jerzy Janowicz (POL) 64 63 67(10) 63; Jarkko Nieminen (FIN) d. Grzegorz Panfil (POL) 64 64 64; Henri Kontinen/Jarkko Nieminen (FIN) d. Mariusz Fyrstenberg/Marcin Matkowski (POL) 76(1) 76(5) 64; Jerzy Janowicz (POL) d. Harri Heliovaara (FIN) 63 64; Grzegorz Panfil (POL) d. Micke Kontinen (FIN) 76(1) 64.

Slovak Republic defeated Ukraine 4-1, Bratislava, Slovak Republic, Clay (O): Martin Klizan (SVK) d. Illya Marchenko (UKR) 67(4) 63 61 63; Sergiy Stakhovsky (UKR) d. Pavol Cervenak (SVK) 75 62 61; Filip Polasek/Igor Zelenay (SVK) d. Sergei Bubka/Sergiy Stakhovsky (UKR) 75 67(3) 62 67(3) 64; Martin Klizan (SVK) d. Sergiy Stakhovsky (UKR) 64 36 76(6) 62; Pavol Cervenak (SVK) d. Artem Smirnov (UKR) 64 64.

Poland and Ukraine relegated to Europe/Africa Zone Group II in 2012.

GROUP II

Americas Zone
First round 4-6 March
Peru defeated Netherlands Antilles 5-0, Lima, Peru, Clay (O): Ivan Miranda (PER) d. David Josepa (AHO) 60 60 61; Mauricio Echazu (PER) d. Alexander Blom (AHO) 62 63 75; Duilio Beretta/Sergio Galdos (PER) d. Alexander Blom/Martijn van Haasteren (AHO) 64 62 36 62; Sergio Galdos (PER) d. David Josepa (AHO) 62 62; Duilio Beretta (PER) d. Nick van Rosberg (AHO) 60 60.

Dominican Republic defeated El Salvador 5-0, Santa Tecla, El Salvador, Clay (O): Jhonson Garcia (DOM) d. Marcelo Arevalo (ESA) 63 63 61; Victor Estrella (DOM) d. Rafael Arevalo (ESA) 26 76(3) 64 61; Victor Estrella/Jose Hernandez (DOM) d. Marcelo Arevalo/Rafael Arevalo (ESA) 64 64 46 64; Luis Delgado (DOM) d. Andres Weisskopf (ESA) 64 62; Jhonson Garcia (DOM) d. Alberto Emmanuel Alvarado Larin (ESA) 60 61.

Paraguay defeated Puerto Rico 4-1, Mayaguez, Puerto Rico, Hard (O): Daniel Lopez (PAR) d. Ricardo Gonzalez-Diaz (PUR) 62 62 64; Alex Llompart (PUR) d. Diego Galeano (PAR) 63 36 46 75 61; Daniel Lopez/Gustavo Ramirez (PAR) d. Chris Brandi/Alex Llompart (PUR) 46 63 61 46 75; Daniel Lopez (PAR) d. Alex Llompart (PUR) 63 60 64; Diego Galeano (PAR) d. Chris Brandi (PUR) 64 63.

Venezuela defeated Haiti 3-2, Caracas, Venezuela, Hard (O): Olivier Sajous (HAI) d. Luis David Martinez (VEN) 76(2) 63 36 64; Piero Luisi (VEN) d. Jean Marc Bazanne (HAI) 62 62 61; Piero Luisi/Roberto Maytin (VEN) d. Joel Allen/Olivier Sajous (HAI) 67(3) 36 76(0) 62 62; Olivier Sajous (HAI) d. Piero Luisi (VEN) 67(3) 64 64 06 64; Roman Recarte (VEN) d. Jean Marc Bazanne (HAI) 63 61 62.

Second round 8-10 July
Peru defeated Dominican Republic 3-1, Lima, Peru, Clay (O): Duilio Beretta (PER) d. Jhonson Garcia (DOM) 63 64 75; Victor Estrella (DOM) d. Ivan Miranda (PER) 64 75 16 64; Duilio Beretta/Sergio Galdos (PER) d. Victor Estrella/Jhonson Garcia (DOM) 64 67(6) 64 63; Duilio Beretta (PER) d. Victor Estrella (DOM) 75 63 67(4) 64.

Paraguay defeated Venezuela 3-1, Asuncion, Paraguay, Clay (O): Diego Galeano (PAR) d. Roman Recarte (VEN) 64 76(3) 63; David Souto (VEN) d. Daniel Lopez (PAR) 76(4) 75 64; Diego Galeano/Daniel Lopez (PAR) d. Piero Luisi/Roberto Maytin (VEN) 46 64 75 62; Diego Galeano (PAR) d. David Souto (VEN) 46 63 64 64.

Third round 16-18 September
Peru defeated Paraguay 3-1, Asuncion, Paraguay, Clay (O): Mauricio Echazu (PER) d. Daniel Lopez (PAR) 76(1) 75 63; Diego Galeano (PAR) d. Duilio Beretta (PER) 16 64 64 64; Duilio Beretta/Sergio Galdos (PER) d. Diego Galeano/Gustavo Ramirez (PAR) 76(5) 46 62 76(5); Duilio Beretta (PER) d. Daniel Lopez (PAR) 60 76(6) 63.

Peru promoted to Americas Zone Group I in 2012.

Relegation play-offs 8-10 July
El Salvador defeated Netherlands Antilles 3-2, Santa Tecla, El Salvador, Clay (O): Alexander Blom (AHO) d. Rafael Arevalo (ESA) 46 61 62 75; Marcelo Arevalo (ESA) d. Martijn van Haasteren (AHO) 61 57 62 76(4); Marcelo Arevalo/Rafael Arevalo (ESA) d. Alexander Blom/Martijn van Haasteren (AHO) 63 62 63; Alexander Blom (AHO) d. Marcelo Arevalo (ESA) 64 64 36 36 63; Rafael Arevalo (ESA) d. Martijn van Haasteren (AHO) 64 62 61.

Puerto Rico defeated Haiti 4-1, Mayaguez, Puerto Rico, Hard (O): Chris Brandi (PUR) d. Gonzales Austin (HAI) 63 64 61; Gabriel Flores Ruiz (PUR) d. Olivier Sajous (HAI) 64 46 61 64; Gilberto Alvarez/Alex Llompart (PUR) d. Joel Allen/Olivier Sajous (HAI) 64 62 64; Chris Brandi (PUR) d. Johann Coles (HAI) 64 63; Gonzales Austin (HAI) d. Gabriel Flores Ruiz (PUR) 76(6) 76(5).

Haiti and Netherlands Antilles relegated to Americas Zone Group III in 2012.

Asia/Oceania Zone
First round 4-6 March
Korea, Rep. defeated Syria 4-1, Changwon, Korea, Rep., Hard (O): Hyun-Joon Kim (KOR) d. Marc Abdulnour (SYR) 63 61 61; Soong-Jae Cho (KOR) d. Issam Al Tawil (SYR) 61 64 61; Soong-Jae Cho/Hyun-Joon Kim (KOR) d. Romain Radwan/Majdi Salim (SYR) 62 61 61; Marc Abdulnour (SYR) d. Suk-Young Jeong (KOR) 36 64 76(3); Yong-Kyu Lim (KOR) d. Issam Al Tawil (SYR) 62 62.

Pakistan defeated Hong Kong, China 3-2, Victoria Park, Hong Kong, China, Hard (O): Hiu-Tung Yu (HKG) d. Aisam Qureshi (PAK) 76(3) 46 67(2) 75 64; Aqeel Khan (PAK) d. Martin Sayer (HKG) 75 75 64; Aqeel Khan/Aisam Qureshi (PAK) d. Jonathan Chu/Coenie van Wyk (HKG) 76(4) 64 64; Aisam Qureshi (PAK) d. Martin Sayer (HKG) 76(8) 63 76(4); Jonathan Chu (HKG) d. Samir Iftikhar (PAK) 61 64.

Indonesia defeated Iran 3-2, Tehran, Iran, Clay (I): Anoosha Shahgholi (IRI) d. Sunu-Wahyu Trijati (INA) 63 64 26 46 75; Christopher Rungkat (INA) d. Shahin Khaledan (IRI) 76(3) 61 63; Christopher Rungkat/Sunu-Wahyu Trijati (INA) d. Anoosha Shahgholi/Omid Souri (IRI) 63 61 75; Christopher Rungkat (INA) d. Mohsen Hossein Zade (IRI) 63 63 60; Shahin Khaledan (IRI) d. Aditya Hari Sasongko (INA) 61 67(5) 63.

Thailand defeated Pacific Oceania 5-0, Guam, Pacific Oceania, Hard (O): Danai Udomchoke (THA) d. Cyril Jacobe (POC) 60 62 63; Kittiphong Wachiramanowong (THA) d. Michael Leong (POC) 63 63 60; Sanchai Ratiwatana/Sonchat Ratiwatana (THA) d. Cyril Jacobe/Leon So'onalole (POC) 64 75 62; Danai Udomchoke (THA) d. Michael Leong (POC) 64 60; Kittiphong Wachiramanowong (THA) d. Cyril Jacobe (POC) 62 62.

Second round 8-10 July
Korea, Rep. defeated Pakistan 4-0, Gimcheon, Korea, Rep., Hard (O): Kyu-Tae Im (KOR) d. Aqeel Khan (PAK) 62 64 62; Yong-Kyu Lim (KOR) d. Aisam Qureshi (PAK) 62 57 64 36 63; Yong-Kyu Lim/Jae-Min Seol (KOR) d. Aqeel Khan/Aisam Qureshi (PAK) 64 62 67(7) 46 1311; Young-Jun Kim (KOR) d. Yasir Khan (PAK) 60 60.

Thailand defeated Indonesia 4-1, Nonthaburi, Thailand, Hard (O): Christopher Rungkat (INA) d. Kittiphong Wachiramanowong (THA) 62 76(3) 60; Danai Udomchoke (THA) d. Elbert Sie (INA) 61 61 60; Sanchai Ratiwatana/Sonchat Ratiwatana (THA) d. Aditya Hari Sasongko/David Agung Susanto (INA) 62 62 62; Danai Udomchoke (THA) d. Christopher Rungkat (INA) 64 62 61; Kittiphong Wachiramanowong (THA) d. Elbert Sie (INA) 67(4) 75 ret.

Third round 16-18 September
Korea, Rep. defeated Thailand 3-0, Gimcheon, Korea, Rep., Hard (O): Yong-Kyu Lim (KOR) d. Perakiat Siriluethaiwattana (THA) 63 63 62; Young-Jun Kim (KOR) d. Kittiphong Wachiramanowong (THA) 62 63 75; Yong-Kyu Lim/Jae-Min Seol (KOR) d. Sanchai Ratiwatana/Sonchat Ratiwatana (THA) 21 ret.; Hong Chung (KOR) v. Kittiphong Wachiramanowong (THA) 46 65 abn.

Korea, Rep. promoted to Asia/Oceania Zone Group I in 2012.

Relegation play-offs 8-10 July
Hong Kong, China defeated Syria 4-1, Victoria Park, Hong Kong, China, Hard (O): Nicholas Sayer (HKG) d. Issam Al Tawil (SYR) 64 36 57 61 63; Hiu-Tung Yu (HKG) d. Marc Abdulnour (SYR) 62 64 63; Jonathan Chu/Coenie van Wyk (HKG) d. Marc Abdulnour/Issam Al Tawil (SYR) 64 16 63 61; Bruno Abdel Nour (SYR) d. Nicholas Sayer (HKG) 62 60; Coenie van Wyk (HKG) d. Romain Radwan (SYR) 61 64.

Pacific Oceania defeated Iran 4-1, Guam, Pacific Oceania, Hard (O): West Nott (POC) d. Shahin Khaledan (IRI) 61 64 62; Michael Leong (POC) d. Rouzbeh Kamran (IRI) 16 63 64 64; Cyril Jacobe/Daniel Llarenas (POC) d. Ashkan Shokoofi/Seyed Akbar Taheri Rahaghi (IRI) 36 63 64 62; Shahin Khaledan (IRI) d. Cyril Jacobe (POC) 64 64; West Nott (POC) d. Rouzbeh Kamran (IRI) 63 64.

Iran and Syria relegated to Asia/Oceania Zone Group III in 2012.

Europe/Africa Zone
First round 4-6 March
Great Britain defeated Tunisia 4-1, Bolton, Great Britain, Hard (I): Malek Jaziri (TUN) d. Jamie Baker (GBR) 46 63 75 62; James Ward (GBR) d. Sami Ghorbel (TUN) 60 62 60; Colin Fleming/Jamie Murray (GBR) d. Slim Hamza/Malek Jaziri (TUN) 61 36 63 64; James Ward (GBR) d. Malek Jaziri (TUN) 36 63 36 63 86; Jamie Baker (GBR) d. Slim Hamza (TUN) 61 64.

Luxembourg defeated Ireland 3-2, Dublin, Ireland, Hard (I): Conor Niland (IRL) d. Mike Vermeer (LUX) 61 60 62; Gilles Muller (LUX) d. Barry King (IRL) 46 61 63 63; Laurent Bram/Gilles Muller (LUX) d. James Cluskey/James McGee (IRL) 76(4) 76(4) 64; Gilles Muller (LUX) d. Conor Niland (IRL) 64 64 64; James McGee (IRL) d. Mike Vermeer (LUX) 61 62.

Belarus defeated Bulgaria 4-1, Minsk, Belarus, Hard (I): Uladzimir Ignatik (BLR) d. Todor Enev (BUL) 62 36 67(4) 62 62; Dimitar Kutrovsky (BUL) d. Siarhei Betau (BLR) 75 64 26 76(2); Uladzimir Ignatik/Max Mirnyi (BLR) d. Valentin Dimov/Dimitar Kuzmanov (BUL) 62 64 64; Uladzimir Ignatik (BLR) d. Dimitar Kutrovsky (BUL) 36 62 61 64; Alexander Bury (BLR) d. Dimitar Kuzmanov (BUL) 62 63.

Hungary defeated Cyprus 5-0, Nicosia, Cyprus, Hard (O): Adam Kellner (HUN) d. Rares Cuzdriorean (CYP) 64 64 63; Attila Balazs (HUN) d. Philippos Tsangaridis (CYP) 61 62 62; Attila Balazs/Kornel Bardoczky (HUN) d. Rares Cuzdriorean/Christopher Koutrouzas (CYP) 61 64 63; Attila Balazs (HUN) d. Sergis Kyratzis (CYP) 64 76(6); Marton Fucsovics (HUN) d. Philippos Tsangaridis (CYP) 64 63.

Bosnia/Herzegovina defeated Morocco 3-2, Marrakech, Morocco, Clay (O): Reda El Amrani (MAR) d. Amer Delic (BIH) 62 76(4) 64; Aldin Setkic (BIH) d. Talal Ouahabi (MAR) 64 26 57 63 64; Amer Delic/Ismar Gorcic (BIH) d. Reda El Amrani/Talal Ouahabi (MAR) 63 62 16 64; Reda El Amrani (MAR) d. Aldin Setkic (BIH) 26 62 60 61; Amer Delic (BIH) d. Talal Ouahabi (MAR) 61 63 46 61.

Estonia defeated Lithuania 3-2, Tallinn, Estonia, Hard (I): Ricardas Berankis (LTU) d. Jaak Poldma (EST) 76(3) 62 63; Jurgen Zopp (EST) d. Laurynas Grigelis (LTU) 45 ret.; Mait Kunnap/Jurgen Zopp (EST) d. Ricardas Berankis/Dovydas Sakinis (LTU) 62 63 36 63; Ricardas Berankis (LTU) d. Jurgen Zopp (EST) 16 46 64 63 119; Jaak Poldma (EST) d. Dovydas Sakinis (LTU) 61 64 16 61.

Denmark defeated Monaco 3-2, Kolding, Denmark, Carpet (I): Jean-Rene Lisnard (MON) d. Martin Pedersen (DEN) 76(3) 46 64 26 62; Frederik Nielsen (DEN) d. Thomas Oger (MON) 75 62 75; Thomas Kromann/Frederik Nielsen (DEN) d. Guillaume Couillard/Jean-Rene Lisnard (MON) 62 63 61; Frederik Nielsen (DEN) d. Jean-Rene Lisnard (MON) 63 62 64; Benjamin Balleret (MON) d. Soren Wedege (DEN) 62 76(5).

Latvia defeated Greece 4-1, Thessaloniki, Greece, Clay (O): Andis Juska (LAT) d. Theodoros Angelinos (GRE) 63 75 62; Deniss Pavlovs (LAT) d. Alexandros Jakupovic (GRE) 63 61 61; Andis Juska/Deniss Pavlovs (LAT) d. Konstantinos Economidis/Alexandros Jakupovic (GRE) 64 63 63; Deniss Pavlovs (LAT) d. Paris Gemouchidis (GRE) 63 64; Konstantinos Economidis (GRE) d. Mikelis Libietis (LAT) 61 62.

Second round 8-10 July
Great Britain defeated Luxembourg 4-1, Glasgow, Great Britain, Hard (I): Gilles Muller (LUX) d. James Ward (GBR) 63 76(4) 61; Andy Murray (GBR) d. Laurent Bram (LUX) 60 60 60; Andy Murray/Jamie Murray (GBR) d. Laurent Bram/Mike Vermeer (LUX) 75 62 60; Andy Murray (GBR) d. Gilles Muller (LUX) 64 63 61; James Ward (GBR) d. Mike Vermeer (LUX) 61 63.

Hungary defeated Belarus 3-2, Godollo, Hungary, Clay (O): Uladzimir Ignatik (BLR) d. Adam Kellner (HUN) 76(5) 64 57 16 75; Attila Balazs (HUN) d. Siarhei Betau (BLR) 62 61 75; Uladzimir Ignatik/Max Mirnyi (BLR) d. Kornel Bardoczky/Marton Fucsovics (HUN) 75 67(4) 67(2) 61 64; Attila Balazs (HUN) d. Uladzimir Ignatik (BLR) 76(5) 63 76(7); Adam Kellner (HUN) d. Siarhei Betau (BLR) 62 60 62.

Bosnia/Herzegovina defeated Estonia 3-2, Tuzla, Bosnia/Herzegovina, Hard (I): Jurgen Zopp (EST) d. Aldin Setkic (BIH) 16 75 63 57 62; Amer Delic (BIH) d. Jaak Poldma (EST) 64 61 75; Amer Delic/Ismar Gorcic (BIH) d. Mait Kunnap/Jurgen Zopp (EST) 64 61 67(1) 26 62; Amer Delic (BIH) d. Jurgen Zopp (EST) 76(12) 63 75; Vladimir Ivanov (EST) d. Tomislav Brkic (BIH) 75 36 63.

Denmark defeated Latvia 3-2, Frederiksberg, Denmark, Clay (O): Andis Juska (LAT) d. Martin Pedersen (DEN) 62 76(3) 26 62; Frederik Nielsen (DEN) d. Martins Podzus (LAT) 06 16 75 63 60; Thomas Kromann/Frederik Nielsen (DEN) d. Andis Juska/Deniss Pavlovs (LAT) 61 36 46 64 62; Andis Juska (LAT) d. Frederik Nielsen (DEN) 61 46 62 62; Martin Pedersen (DEN) d. Martins Podzus (LAT) 62 64 61.

Third round 16-18 September
Great Britain defeated Hungary 5-0, Glasgow, Great Britain, Hard (I): James Ward (GBR) d. Attila Balazs (HUN) 64 64 46 64; Andy Murray (GBR) d. Sebo Kiss (HUN) 60 62 76(3); Colin Fleming/Ross Hutchins (GBR) d. Attila Balazs/Kornel Bardoczky (HUN) 63 64 64; Andy Murray (GBR) d. Gyorgy Balazs (HUN) 76(3) 63; Colin Fleming (GBR) d. Sebo Kiss (HUN) 64 63.

Denmark defeated Bosnia/Herzegovina 3-2, Hillerod, Denmark, Hard (I): Frederik Nielsen (DEN) d. Aldin Setkic (BIH) 64 62 63; Amer Delic (BIH) d. Martin Pedersen (DEN) 61 67(5) 76(1) 46 64; Thomas Kromann/Frederik Nielsen (DEN) d. Amer Delic/Ismar Gorcic (BIH) 36 62 63 36 63; Amer Delic (BIH) d. Frederik Nielsen (DEN) 76(5) 75 63; Martin Pedersen (DEN) d. Damir Dzumhur (BIH) 36 61 64 61.

Bosnia/Herzegovina and Great Britain promoted to Europe/Africa Zone Group I in 2012.

Relegation play-offs 8-10 July
Ireland defeated Tunisia 3-2, Dublin, Ireland, Hard (I): Conor Niland (IRL) d. Anis Ghorbel (TUN) 64 62 61; Malek Jaziri (TUN) d. Barry King (IRL) 61 61 75; Anis Ghorbel/Malek Jaziri (TUN) d. James Cluskey/Conor Niland (IRL) 64 76(4) 76(5); Conor Niland (IRL) d. Malek Jaziri (TUN) 75 75 61; Barry King (IRL) d. Anis Ghorbel (TUN) 76(7) 62 61.

Cyprus defeated Bulgaria 3-2, Sofia, Bulgaria, Carpet (I): Marcos Baghdatis (CYP) d. Tzvetan Mihov (BUL) 61 64 61; Dimitar Kutrovsky (BUL) d. Philippos Tsangaridis (CYP) 60 62 62; Marcos Baghdatis/Rares Cuzdriorean (CYP) d. Todor Enev/Dimitar Kutrovsky (BUL) 62 62 36 46 64; Marcos Baghdatis (CYP) d. Dimitar Kutrovsky (BUL) 63 36 76(3) 75; Dimitar Kuzmanov (BUL) d. Christopher Koutrouzas (CYP) 62 61.

Morocco defeated Lithuania 5-0, Vilnius, Lithuania, Clay (O): Reda El Amrani (MAR) d. Lukas Mugevicius (LTU) 75 61 61; Yassine Idmbarek (MAR) d. Dovydas Sakinis (LTU) 26 62 63 20 ret.; Anas Fattar/Hicham Khaddari (MAR) d. Lukas Mugevicius/Dovydas Sakinis (LTU) 64 64 36 62; Hicham Khaddari (MAR) d. Julius Tverijonas (LTU) 64 63; Yassine Idmbarek (MAR) d. Julius Gotovskis (LTU) 16 64 62.

Monaco defeated Greece 3-2, Thessaloniki, Greece, Clay (O): Jean-Rene Lisnard (MON) d. Alexandros Jakupovic (GRE) 62 36 75 64; Benjamin Balleret (MON) d. Theodoros Angelinos (GRE) 36 76(5) 64 64; Guillaume Couillard/Thomas Oger (MON) d. Konstantinos Economidis/Alexandros Jakupovic (GRE) 36 62 76(5) 26 62; Konstantinos Economidis (GRE) d. Benjamin Balleret (MON) 63 76(4); Theodoros Angelinos (GRE) d. Jean-Rene Lisnard (MON) 76(3) 61.

Bulgaria, Greece, and Lithuania are relegated to Europe Zone Group III in 2012. Tunisia is relegated to Africa Zone Group III in 2012.

GROUP III

Africa Zone
Date: 4-9 July
Venue: Cairo, Egypt
Surface: Clay (O)

Group A 4 July Madagascar defeated Benin 2-1: Lofo Ramiaramanana (MAD) d. Christophe Pognon (BEN) 64 64; Alexis Klegou (BEN) d. Antso Rakotondramanga (MAD) 63 62; Antso Rakotondramanga/Lofo Ramiaramanana (MAD) d. Christophe Pognon/Alexis Klegou (BEN) 64 64. **Egypt defeated Rwanda w/o.**

5 July Egypt defeated Benin 3-0: Sherif Sabry (EGY) d. Magloire Yakpa (BEN) 61 61; Mohamed Safwat (EGY) d. Alexis Klegou (BEN) 75 62; Karim-Mohamed Maamoun/Sherif Sabry (EGY) d. Tunde Segodo/Alexis Klegou (BEN) 76(3) 62. **Madagascar defeated Rwanda w/o.**

6 July Egypt defeated Nigeria 3-0: Sherif Sabry (EGY) d. Lawal Shehu (NGR) 63 62; Mohamed Safwat (EGY) d. Abdul-Mumin Babalola (NGR) 62 64; Sherif Sabry/Mohamed Safwat (EGY) d. Abdul-Mumin Babalola/Lawal Shehu (NGR) 62 76(1). **Benin defeated Rwanda w/o.**

7 July Madagascar defeated Nigeria 2-1: Jacob Rasolondrazana (MAD) d. Sunday Emmanuel (NGR) 75 64; Abdul-Mumin Babalola (NGR) d. Antso Rakotondramanga (MAD) 75 75; Antso Rakotondramanga/Lofo Ramiaramanana (MAD) d. Abdul-Mumin Babalola/Lawal Shehu (NGR) 36 64 63. **Nigeria defeated Rwanda w/o.**

8 July Egypt defeated Madagascar 3-0: Sherif Sabry (EGY) d. Jacob Rasolondrazana (MAD) 63 64; Mohamed Safwat (EGY) d. Lofo Ramiaramanana (MAD) 64 46 61; Karim-Mohamed Maamoun/Mohamed Safwat (EGY) d. Antso Rakotondramanga/Jacob Rasolondrazana (MAD) 63 63. **Benin defeated Nigeria 3-0:** Christophe Pognon (BEN) d. Sunday Emmanuel (NGR) 75 75; Alexis Klegou (BEN) d. Abdul-Mumin Babalola (NGR) 26 61 62; Tunde Segodo/Magloire Yakpa (BEN) d. Abdul-Mumin Babalola/Sunday Emmanuel (NGR) 61 60.

Group A final positions: 1. Egypt, 2. Madagascar, 3. Benin, 4. Nigeria, 5. Rwanda.

Group B 4 July Algeria defeated Kenya 3-0: Sid Ali Akili (ALG) d. Dennis Ochieng (KEN) 61 61; Abdelhak Hameurlaine (ALG) d. Francis Thuku Mwangi (KEN) 60 61; Mohamed Amine Kerroum/Mohamed-Redha Ouahab (ALG) d. Gilbert Kibet/Ismael Changawa Ruwa (KEN) 62 62. **Zimbabwe defeated Cote D'Ivoire 2-1:** Mark Fynn (ZIM) d. Valentin Sanon (CIV) 75 60; Terence Nugent (CIV) d. Takanyi Garanganga (ZIM) 75 64; Mark Fynn/Takanyi Garanganga (ZIM) d. Terence Nugent/Aboubacar Sigue (CIV) 16 63 76(5).

5 July Algeria defeated Cote D'Ivoire 2-1: Sid Ali Akili (ALG) d. Aboubacar Sigue (CIV) 75 67(6) 64; Terence Nugent (CIV) d. Abdelhak Hameurlaine (ALG) 46 63 62; Abdelhak Hameurlaine/Mohamed-Redha Ouahab (ALG) d. Terence Nugent/Aboubacar Sigue (CIV) 67(6) 61 63. **Ghana defeated Kenya 3-0:** Raymond Hayford (GHA) d. Dennis Ochieng (KEN) 61 61; Emmanuel Mensah (GHA) d. Francis Thuku Mwangi (KEN) 61 60; Robert Mensah Kpodo/Emmanuel Mensah (GHA) d. Gilbert Kibet/Francis Thuku Mwangi (KEN) 62 61.

6 July Algeria defeated Ghana 2-1: Sid Ali Akili (ALG) d. Raymond Hayford (GHA) 75 61; Abdelhak Hameurlaine (ALG) d. Emmanuel Mensah (GHA) 64 61; Robert Mensah Kpodo/Emmanuel Mensah (GHA) d. Mohamed Amine Kerroum/Mohamed-Redha Ouahab (ALG) 75 61. **Zimbabwe defeated Kenya 3-0:** Benjamin Lock (ZIM) d. Gilbert Kibet (KEN) 61 61; Takanyi Garanganga (ZIM) d. Francis Thuku Mwangi (KEN) 61 63; Mark Fynn/Benjamin Lock (ZIM) d. Dennis Ochieng/Ismael Changawa Ruwa (KEN) 60 61.

7 July Zimbabwe defeated Ghana 3-0: Mark Fynn (ZIM) d. Raymond Hayford (GHA) 60 61; Takanyi Garanganga (ZIM) d. Emmanuel Mensah (GHA) 63 64; Mark Fynn/Benjamin Lock (ZIM) d. Robert Mensah Kpodo/Emmanuel Mensah (GHA) 62 75. **Cote D'Ivoire defeated Kenya 3-0:** Aboubacar Sigue (CIV) d. Gilbert Kibet (KEN) 60 46 60; Terence Nugent (CIV) d. Dennis Ochieng (KEN) 62 63; Lavry Sylvain N'Yaba/Aboubacar Sigue (CIV) d. Francis Thuku Mwangi/Ismael Changawa Ruwa (KEN) 61 46 75.

8 July Algeria defeated Zimbabwe 2-1: Sid Ali Akili (ALG) d. Mark Fynn (ZIM) 64 64; Abdelhak Hameurlaine (ALG) d. Takanyi Garanganga (ZIM) 64 64; Mark Fynn/Benjamin Lock (ZIM) d. Mohamed Amine Kerroum/Mohamed-Redha Ouahab (ALG) 62 63. **Ghana defeated Cote D'Ivoire 2-1:** Aboubacar Sigue (CIV) d. Raymond Hayford (GHA) 57 63 76(4); Emmanuel Mensah (GHA) d. Lavry Sylvain N'Yaba (CIV) 61 67(8) 63; Robert Mensah Kpodo/Emmanuel Mensah (GHA) d. Lavry Sylvain N'Yaba/Aboubacar Sigue (CIV) 61 64.

Group B final positions: 1. Algeria, 2. Zimbabwe, 3. Ghana, 4. Cote D'Ivoire, 5. Kenya.

Play-off for 1st/4th positions:
9 July Egypt defeated Zimbabwe 2-0: Sherif Sabry (EGY) d. Benjamin Lock (ZIM) 60 63; Mohamed Safwat (EGY) d. Takanyi Garanganga (ZIM) 62 75; doubles not played.
Madagascar defeated Algeria 2-1: Jacob Rasolondrazana (MAD) d. Sid Ali Akili (ALG) 36 75 62; Abdelhak Hameurlaine (ALG) d. Lofo Ramiaramanana (MAD) 36 63 60; Antso Rakotondramanga/Jacob Rasolondrazana (MAD) d. Abdelhak Hameurlaine/Mohamed-Redha Ouahab (ALG) 61 61.

Play-off for 5th/6th position:
9 July Benin defeated Ghana 3-0: Tunde Segodo (BEN) d. Raymond Hayford (GHA) 64 75; Alexis Klegou (BEN) d. Emmanuel Mensah (GHA) 62 46 61; Tunde Segodo/Magloire Yakpa (BEN) d. Japheth Anwasiba Bagerbaseh/Robert Mensah Kpodo (GHA) 63 62.

Play-off for 7th/8th position:
9 July Nigeria defeated Cote D'Ivoire 2-1: Aboubacar Sigue (CIV) d. Henry Atseye (NGR) 46 61 64; Lawal Shehu (NGR) d. Lavry Sylvain N'Yaba (CIV) 64 61; Henry Atseye/Lawal Shehu (NGR) d. Lavry Sylvain N'Yaba/Aboubacar Sigue (CIV) 61 64.

Play-off for 9th/10th position:
9 July Kenya defeated Rwanda w/o.

Final positions: 1=. Egypt, Madagascar, 3=. Algeria, Zimbabwe, 5. Benin, 6. Ghana, 7. Nigeria, 8. Cote D'Ivoire, 9. Kenya, 10. Rwanda.

Egypt and Madagascar promoted to Europe/Africa Zone Group II in 2012.

Americas Zone
Date: 15-19 June
Venue: Santa Cruz, Bolivia
Surface: Clay (O)

Group A 15 June Guatemala defeated Honduras 3-0: Julen Uriguen (GUA) d. Keny Turcios (HON) 62 62; Christopher Diaz-Figueroa (GUA) d. Alejandro Obando (HON) 63 60; Wilfredo Gonzalez/Sebastien Vidal (GUA) d. Ricardo Lau Cooper/Ricardo Pineda (HON) 64 61. **Costa Rica defeated Jamaica 3-0:** Pablo Nunez (CRC) d. Dwayne Pagon (JAM) 64 76(5); Ignaci Roca (CRC) d. Brandon Burke (JAM) 64 64; Pablo Nunez/Ignaci Roca (CRC) d. Brandon Burke/Macoy Malcolm (JAM) 62 62.

16 June Guatemala defeated Jamaica 3-0: Julen Uriguen (GUA) d. Macoy Malcolm (JAM) 61 61; Christopher Diaz-Figueroa (GUA) d. Brandon Burke (JAM) 61 63; Wilfredo Gonzalez/Sebastien Vidal (GUA) d. Atton Burrell/Dwayne Pagon (JAM) 60 62. **Costa Rica defeated Honduras 2-1:** Keny Turcios (HON) d. Pablo Nunez (CRC) 61 76(4); Ignaci Roca (CRC) d. Alejandro Obando (HON) 63 62; Pablo Nunez/Ignaci Roca (CRC) d. Ricardo Pineda/Keny Turcios (HON) 76(5) 63.

17 June Guatemala defeated Costa Rica 3-0: Julen Uriguen (GUA) d. Pablo Nunez (CRC) 61 63; Christopher Diaz-Figueroa (GUA) d. Ignaci Roca (CRC) 60 61; Christopher Diaz-Figueroa/Julen Uriguen (GUA) d. Pablo Nunez/Ignaci Roca (CRC) 62 46 61. **Jamaica defeated Honduras 2-1:** Ricardo Lau Cooper (HON) d. Dwayne Pagon (JAM) 46 61 61; Brandon Burke (JAM) d. Keny Turcios (HON) 26 64 63; Brandon Burke/Macoy Malcolm (JAM) d. Alejandro Obando/Ricardo Pineda (HON) 61 76(4).

Group A final positions: 1. Guatemala, 2. Costa Rica, 3. Jamaica, 4. Honduras.

Group B 15 June Bahamas defeated Aruba 3-0: Devin Mullings (BAH) d. Gian Hodgson (ARU) 64 60; Marvin Rolle (BAH) d. Ibian Hodgson (ARU) 63 62; Jamaal Adderley/Marvin Rolle (BAH) d. Mitchell de Jong/Gian Hodgson (ARU) 63 62. **Barbados defeated Bolivia 2-1:** Haydn Lewis (BAR) d. Mauricio Doria-Medina (BOL) 63 64; Darian King (BAR) d. Federico Zeballos (BOL) 46 64 63; Mauricio Doria-Medina/Federico Zeballos (BOL) d. Anthony Marshall/Seannon Williams (BAR) 62 61.

16 June Bolivia defeated Bahamas 3-0: Mauricio Doria-Medina (BOL) d. Devin Mullings (BAH) 63 64; Federico Zeballos (BOL) d. Marvin Rolle (BAH) 64 61; Mauricio Doria-Medina/Federico Zeballos (BOL) d. Jamaal Adderley/Marvin Rolle (BAH) 63 62. **Barbados defeated Aruba 3-0:** Haydn Lewis (BAR) d. Gian Hodgson (ARU) 62 62; Darian King (BAR) d. Ibian Hodgson (ARU) 61 63; Darian King/Haydn Lewis (BAR) d. Mitchell de Jong/Gian Hodgson (ARU) 60 61.

17 June Barbados defeated Bahamas 2-1: Haydn Lewis (BAR) d. Devin Mullings (BAH) 63 76(5); Darian King (BAR) d. Marvin Rolle (BAH) 62 61; Jamaal Adderley/Timothy Neilly (BAH) d. Anthony Marshall/Seannon Williams (BAR) 63 64. **Bolivia defeated Aruba 3-0:** Mauricio Doria-Medina (BOL) d. Gian Hodgson (ARU) 61 60; Federico Zeballos (BOL) d. Mitchell de Jong (ARU) 62 61; Boris Arias/Hugo Dellien (BOL) d. Mitchell de Jong/Gian Hodgson (ARU) 62 63.

Group B final positions: 1. Barbados, 2. Bolivia, 3. Bahamas, 4. Aruba.

Play-off for 1st/4th positions:
Results carried forward: Guatemala defeated Costa Rica 3-0; Barbados defeated Bolivia 2-1.
18 June Bolivia defeated Guatemala 2-1: Hugo Dellien (BOL) d. Julen Uriguen (GUA) 64 67(3) 63; Christopher Diaz-Figueroa (GUA) d. Federico Zeballos (BOL) 64 75; Mauricio Doria-Medina/Federico Zeballos (BOL) d. Christopher Diaz-Figueroa/Sebastien Vidal (GUA) 61 61. **Barbados defeated Costa Rica 3-0:** Haydn Lewis (BAR) d. Pablo Nunez (CRC) 60 62; Darian King (BAR) d. Ignaci Roca (CRC) 63 62; Darian King/Haydn Lewis (BAR) d. Martin Echandi/Ignaci Roca (CRC) 64 75.

19 June Guatemala defeated Barbados 2-1: Haydn Lewis (BAR) d. Julen Uriguen (GUA) 60 63; Christopher Diaz-Figueroa (GUA) d. Darian King (BAR) 64 16 64; Christopher Diaz-Figueroa/Julen Uriguen (GUA) d. Darian King/Haydn Lewis (BAR) 76(4) 46 64. **Bolivia defeated Costa Rica 3-0:** Hugo Dellien (BOL) d. Pablo Nunez (CRC) 61 64; Mauricio Doria-Medina (BOL) d. Ignaci Roca (CRC) 60 63; Mauricio Doria-Medina/Federico Zeballos (BOL) d. Pablo Nunez/Ignaci Roca (CRC) 62 61.

Relegation play-offs:
Results carried forward: Jamaica defeated Honduras 2-1; Bahamas defeated Aruba 3-0.
18 June Aruba defeated Jamaica 2-1: Gian Hodgson (ARU) d. Macoy Malcolm (JAM) 64 64; Brandon Burke (JAM) d. Mitchell de Jong (ARU) 46 63 61; Mitchell De Jong/Gian Hodgson (ARU) d. Brandon Burke/Macoy Malcolm (JAM) 61 36 64. **Honduras defeated Bahamas 2-1:** Devin Mullings (BAH) d. Ricardo Pineda (HON) 62 62; Ricardo Lau Cooper (HON) d. Marvin Rolle (BAH) 75 62; Jamaal Adderley/Marvin Rolle (BAH) d. Alejandro Obando/Keny Turcios (HON) 63 61.

19 June Bahamas defeated Jamaica 3-0: Timothy Neilly (BAH) d. Atton Burrell (JAM) 62 60; Devin Mullings (BAH) d. Macoy Malcolm (JAM) 60 60; Jamaal Adderley/Devin Mullings (BAH) d. Brandon Burke/Atton Burrell (JAM) 61 60. **Aruba defeated Honduras 2-1:** Gian Hodgson (ARU) d. Ricardo Lau Cooper (HON) 26 63 76(7); Keny Turcios (HON) d. Ibian Hodgson (ARU) 46 63 62; Mitchell de Jong/Gian Hodgson (ARU) d. Ricardo Pineda/Keny Turcios (HON) 63 64.

Final positions: 1. Barbados, 2. Bolivia, 3. Guatemala, 4. Costa Rica, 5. Bahamas, 6. Aruba, 7. Jamaica, 8. Honduras.

Barbados and Bolivia promoted to Americas Zone Group II in 2012. Honduras and Jamaica relegated to Americas Zone Group IV in 2012.

Asia/Oceania Zone
Date: 15-19 June
Venue: Colombo, Sri Lanka
Surface: Hard (O)

Group A 15 June Kuwait defeated Myanmar 3-0: Mohammad Ghareeb (KUW) d. Zaw-Zaw Latt (MYA) 62 62; Abdullah Maqdas (KUW) d. Phyo Min Thar (MYA) 61 60; Mohammad Ghareeb/Abdullah Maqdas (KUW) d. Nge Hnaung/Zaw-Zaw Latt (MYA) 61 60. **Sri Lanka defeated Vietnam 3-0:** Oshada Wijemanne (SRI) d. Quoc-Khanh Le (VIE) 63 64; Harshana Godamanna (SRI) d. Thanh-Hoang Tran (VIE) 61 64; Harshana Godamanna/Rajeev Rajapakse (SRI) d. Quoc-Khanh Le/Quang-Huy Ngo (VIE) 61 67(4) 75.

16 June Vietnam defeated Kuwait 2-1: Minh-Quan Do (VIE) d. Ali Ghareeb (KUW) 26 63 60; Abdullah Maqdas (KUW) d. Thanh-Hoang Tran (VIE) 62 76(2); Quoc-Khanh Le/Quang-Huy Ngo (VIE) d. Mohammad Ghareeb/Abdullah Maqdas (KUW) 62 76(3). **Sri Lanka defeated Myanmar 3-0:** Oshada Wijemanne (SRI) d. Phyo Min Thar (MYA) 62 61; Harshana Godamanna (SRI) d. Nge Hnaung (MYA) 64 62; Harshana Godamanna/Rajeev Rajapakse (SRI) d. Zaw-Zaw Latt/Phyo Min Thar (MYA) 64 63.

17 June Sri Lanka defeated Kuwait 2-1: Mohammad Ghareeb (KUW) d. Oshada Wijemanne (SRI) 75 64; Harshana Godamanna (SRI) d. Abdullah Maqdas (KUW) 54 ret.; Harshana Godamanna/Rajeev Rajapakse (SRI) d. Abdulrahman Alawadhi/Mohammad Ghareeb (KUW) 63 61. **Vietnam defeated Myanmar 2-1:** Minh-Quan Do (VIE) d. Zaw-Zaw Latt (MYA) 60 62; Nge Hnaung (MYA) d. Thanh-Hoang Tran (VIE) 64 62; Minh-Quan Do/Quoc-Khanh Le (VIE) d. Nge Hnaung/Zaw-Zaw Latt (MYA) 61 60.

Group A final positions: 1. Sri Lanka, 2. Vietnam, 3. Kuwait, 4. Myanmar.

Group B 15 June Malaysia defeated United Arab Emirates 2-1: Yew-Ming Si (MAS) d. Hamad Abbas Janahi (UAE) 36 62 63; Omar Awadhy (UAE) d. Ariez Elyaas Deen Heshaam (MAS) 63 67(4) 62; Ahmed Deedat Abdul Razak/Yew-Ming Si (MAS) d. Omar Awadhy/Hamad Abbas Janahi (UAE) 62 62. **Lebanon defeated Oman 2-1:** Karim Alayli (LIB) d. Mohammed Al Nabhani (OMA) 61 75; Bassam Beidas (LIB) d. Khalid Al Nabhani (OMA) 62 61; Khalid Al Nabhani/Mohammed Al Nabhani (OMA) d. Bassam Beidas/Patrick Chucri (LIB) 67(5) 12 ret.

16 June Malaysia defeated Oman 2-1: Mohammed Al Nabhani (OMA) d. Mohamed Nazim Khan (MAS) 61 ret.; Ariez Elyaas Deen Heshaam (MAS) d. Khalid Al Nabhani (OMA) 64 64; Ahmed Deedat Abdul Razak/Yew-Ming Si (MAS) d. Khalid Al Nabhani/Mohammed Al Nabhani (OMA) 36 63 62. **Lebanon defeated United Arab Emirates 2-1:** Karim Alayli (LIB) d. Faisal Bastaki (UAE) 61 61; Bassam Beidas (LIB) d. Khaled Al Hassani (UAE) 62 60; Khaled Al Hassani/Faisal Bastaki (UAE) d. Bassam Beidas/Giovani Samaha (LIB) 43 ret.

17 June Lebanon defeated Malaysia 3-0: Karim Alayli (LIB) d. Ahmed Deedat Abdul Razak (MAS) 62 62; Bassam Beidas (LIB) d. Ariez Elyaas Deen Heshaam (MAS) 61 75; Bassam Beidas/Patrick Chucri (LIB) d. Ariez Elyaas Deen Heshaam/Yew-Ming Si (MAS) 36 61 41 ret. **Oman defeated United Arab Emirates 2-1:** Mohammed Al Nabhani (OMA) d. Hamad Abbas Janahi (UAE) 62 62; Omar Awadhy (UAE) d. Khalid Al Nabhani (OMA) 63 63; Khalid Al Nabhani/Mohammed Al Nabhani (OMA) d. Omar Awadhy/Hamad Abbas Janahi (UAE) 76(4) 26 76(5).

Group B final positions: 1. Lebanon, 2. Malaysia, 3. Oman, 4. United Arab Emirates.

Play-off for 1st/4th positions:
Results carried forward: Sri Lanka defeated Vietnam 3-0; Lebanon defeated Malaysia 3-0.
18 June Sri Lanka defeated Malaysia 2-1: Oshada Wijemanne (SRI) d. Yew-Ming Si (MAS) 64 75; Harshana Godamanna (SRI) d. Ariez Elyaas Deen Heshaam (MAS) 61 62; Ahmed Deedat Abdul Razak/Yew-Ming Si (MAS) d. Rajeev Rajapakse/Dineshkanthan Thangarajah (SRI) 64 62. **Lebanon defeated Vietnam 3-0:** Karim Alayli (LIB) d. Quoc-Khanh Le (VIE) 63 62; Bassam Beidas (LIB) d. Minh-Quan Do (VIE) 60 62; Bassam Beidas/Patrick Chucri (LIB) d. Quoc-Khanh Le/Quang-Huy Ngo (VIE) 45 ret.

19 June Sri Lanka defeated Lebanon 3-0: Oshada Wijemanne (SRI) d. Karim Alayli (LIB) 52 ret.; Harshana Godamanna (SRI) d. Giovani Samaha (LIB) 62 61; Rajeev Rajapakse/Oshada Wijemanne (SRI) d. Patrick Chucri/Giovani Samaha (LIB) 10 ret. **Vietnam defeated Malaysia 2-1:** Yew-Ming Si (MAS) d. Quoc-Khanh Le (VIE) 63 63; Thanh-Hoang Tran (VIE) d. Ariez Elyaas Deen Heshaam (MAS) 26 63 60; Minh-Quan Do/Quang-Huy Ngo (VIE) d. Ahmed Deedat Abdul Razak/Yew-Ming Si (MAS) 60 76(4).

Relegation play-offs:
Results carried forward: Kuwait defeated Myanmar 3-0; Oman defeated United Arab Emirates 2-1.
18 June Kuwait defeated United Arab Emirates 3-0: Mohammad Ghareeb (KUW) d. Hamad Abbas Janahi (UAE) 64 26 62; Abdullah Maqdas (KUW) d. Omar Awadhy (UAE) 61 76(6); Abdulrahman Alawadhi/Ali Ghareeb (KUW) d. Khalid Al Hassani/Faisal Bastaki (UAE) 64 61. **Oman defeated Myanmar 2-1:** Mohammed Al Nabhani (OMA) d. Phyo Min Thar (MYA) 64 63; Khalid Al Nabhani (OMA) d. Nge Hnaung (MYA) 63 63; Zaw-Zaw Latt/Phyo Min Thar (MYA) d. Abdulmalik Alawfi/Khalid Al Nabhani (OMA) 60 60.

19 June Kuwait defeated Oman 3-0: Abdulrahman Alawadhi (KUW) d. Khalid Hamdi Al-Barwani (OMA) 61 61; Ali Ghareeb (KUW) d. Abdulmalik Alawfi (OMA) 61 62; Abdulrahman Alawadhi/Ali Ghareeb (KUW) d. Abdulmalik Alawfi/Khalid Hamdi Al-Barwani (OMA) 60 61. **United Arab Emirates defeated Myanmar 2-1:** Hamad Abbas Janahi (UAE) d. Aung Kyaw Naing (MYA) 62 60; Omar Awadhy (UAE) d. Phyo Min Thar (MYA) 63 36 61; Nge Hnaung/Zaw-Zaw Latt (MYA) d. Faisal Bastaki/Khaled Al Hassani (UAE) 60 60.

Final positions: 1. Sri Lanka, 2. Lebanon, 3. Vietnam, 4. Malaysia, 5. Kuwait, 6. Oman, 7. United Arab Emirates, 8. Myanmar.

Lebanon and Sri Lanka promoted to Asia/Oceania Zone Group II in 2012. Myanmar and United Arab Emirates relegated to Asia/Oceania Zone Group IV in 2012.

Europe Zone
Date: 11-14 May
Venue: Skopje, FYR Macedonia
Surface: Clay (O)

Group A 11 May FYR Macedonia defeated San Marino 3-0: Predrag Rusevski (MKD) d. Giacomo Zonzini (SMR) 60 60; Tomislav Jotovski (MKD) d. Alberto Brighi (SMR) 61 60; Lazar Magdinchev/Predrag Rusevski (MKD) d. Alberto Brighi/Giacomo Zonzini (SMR) 64 61.

12 May Andorra defeated San Marino 2-1: Giacomo Zonzini (SMR) d. Damien Gelabert (AND) 64 61; Jean-Baptiste Poux-Gautier (AND) d. Marco de Rossi (SMR) 61 60; Damien Gelabert/Jean-Baptiste Poux-Gautier (AND) d. Alberto Brighi/Giacomo Zonzini (SMR) 61 61.

13 May FYR Macedonia defeated Andorra 2-1: Dimitar Grabuloski (MKD) d. Damien Gelabert (AND) 61 62; Jean-Baptiste Poux-Gautier (AND) d. Tomislav Jotovski (MKD) 64 62; Lazar Magdinchev/Predrag Rusevski (MKD) d. Damien Gelabert/Jean-Baptiste Poux-Gautier (AND) 63 64.

Group A final positions: 1. FYR Macedonia, 2. Andorra, 3. San Marino.

Group B 11 May Turkey defeated Albania 3-0 : Ergun Zorlu (TUR) d. Flavio Dece (ALB) 60 60; Marsel Ilhan (TUR) d. Ivo Spathari (ALB) 60 60; Haluk Akkoyun/Tuna Altuna (TUR) d. Ferat Istrefi/Ivo Spathari (ALB) 61 61.

12 May Norway defeated Albania 3-0: Stian Boretti (NOR) d. Flavio Dece (ALB) 60 61; Erling Tveit (NOR) d. Ivo Spathari (ALB) 60 60; Stian Boretti/Erling Tveit (NOR) d. Flavio Dece/Ferat Istrefi (ALB) 62 62.

13 May Turkey defeated Norway 2-1: Stian Boretti (NOR) d. Haluk Akkoyun (TUR) 64 63; Marsel Ilhan (TUR) d. Erling Tveit (NOR) 61 61; Marsel Ilhan/Ergun Zorlu (TUR) d. Stian Boretti/Erling Tveit (NOR) 64 26 76(5).

Group B final positions: 1. Turkey, 2. Norway, 3. Albania.

Group C 11 May Montenegro defeated Georgia 3-0: Ljubomir Celebic (MNE) d. George Tsivadze (GEO) 63 76(4); Goran Tosic (MNE) d. Aleksandre Metreveli (GEO) 62 60; Ljubomir Celebic/Goran Tosic (MNE) d. Aleksandre Metreveli/George Tsivadze (GEO) 75 60.

12 May Armenia defeated Georgia 2-1: Daniil Proskura (ARM) d. George Tsivadze (GEO) 64 06 63; Aleksandre Metreveli (GEO) d. Khachatur Khachatryan (ARM) 62 60; Khachatur Khachatryan/Daniil Proskura (ARM) d. NIka Dolidze/Aleksandre Metreveli (GEO) 63 61.

13 May Montenegro defeated Armenia 2-1: Daniil Proskura (ARM) d. Ljubomir Celebic (MNE) 76(2) 62; Goran Tosic (MNE) d. Khachatur Khachatryan (ARM) 60 60; Ljubomir Celebic/Goran Tosic (MNE) d. Khachatur Khachatryan/Daniil Proskura (ARM) 62 62.

Group C final positions: 1. Montenegro, 2. Armenia, 3. Georgia.

Group D 11 May Moldova defeated Malta 3-0: Andrei Gorban (MDA) d. Denzil Agius (MLT) 60 60; Radu Albot (MDA) d. Matthew Asciak (MLT) 75 62; Andrei Gorban/Roman Tudoreanu (MDA) d. Matthew Asciak/Bradley Callus (MLT) 61 60.

12 May Iceland defeated Malta 2-1: Arnar Sigurdsson (ISL) d. Bradley Callus (MLT) 61 61; Matthew Asciak (MLT) d. Andri Jonsson (ISL) 62 61; Andri Jonsson/Arnar Sigurdsson (ISL) d. Matthew Asciak/Mark Gatt (MLT) 76(6) 64.

13 May Moldova defeated Iceland 3-0: Andrei Gorban (MDA) d. Leifur Sigurdarson (ISL) 60 64; Radu Albot (MDA) d. Birkir Gunnarsson (ISL) 60 60; Radu Albot/Andrei Gorban (MDA) d. Andri Jonsson/Jon-Axel Jonsson (ISL) 62 62.

Group D final positions: 1. Moldova, 2. Iceland, 3. Malta.

Play-offs for 1st/4th positions:
14 May Turkey defeated FYR Macedonia 2-0: Ergun Zorlu (TUR) d. Predrag Rusevski (MKD) 36 62 62; Marsel Ilhan (TUR) d. Tomislav Jotovski (MKD) 61 61; doubles not played. **Moldova defeated Montenegro 2-1:** Andrei Gorban (MDA) d. Ljubomir Celebic (MNE) 62 63; Radu Albot (MDA) d. Goran Tosic (MNE) 63 76(7); Ljubomir Celebic/Goran Tosic (MNE) d. Radu Albot/Andrei Gorban (MDA) w/o.

Play-offs for 5th/8th positions:
14 May Norway defeated Andorra 3-0: Stian Boretti (NOR) d. Gerard Blasi-Font (AND) 60 61; Erling Tveit (NOR) d. Jean-Baptiste Poux-Gautier (AND) 76(4) 63; Joachim Bjerke/Oystein Steiro (NOR) d. Gerard Blasi-Font/Damien Gelabert (AND) 61 64.
Armenia defeated Iceland 2-1: Daniil Proskura (ARM) d. Jon-Axel Jonsson (ISL) 61 60; Arnar Sigurdsson (ISL) d. Torgom Asatryan (ARM) 60 64; Khachatur Khachatryan/Daniil Proskura (ARM) d. Andri Jonsson/Arnar Sigurdsson (ISL) 26 63 61.

Play-offs for 9th/12th positions:
14 May Georgia defeated Malta 3-0: George Tsivadze (GEO) d. Denzil Agius (MLT) 62 60; Aleksandre Metreveli (GEO) d. Mark Gatt (MLT) 61 60; Aleksandre Metreveli/Nika Dolidze (GEO) d. Denzil Agius/Mark Gatt (MLT) 60 63. **San Marino defeated Albania 2-1:** Diego Zonzini (SMR) d. Flavio Dece (ALB) 57 63 76(1); Ferat Istrefi (ALB) d. Alberto Brighi (SMR) 76(3) 64; Marco de Rossi/Diego Zonzini (SMR) d. Flavio Dece/Ferat Istrefi (ALB) 64 63.

Final positions: 1=. Moldova, Turkey, 3=. FYR Macedonia, Montenegro, 5=. Armenia, Norway, 7=. Andorra, Iceland, 9=. Georgia, San Marino, 11=. Albania, Malta.

Moldova and Turkey promoted to Europe/Africa Zone Group II in 2012.

GROUP IV

Asia/Oceania Zone
Date: 13-16 April
Venue: Dhaka, Bangladesh
Surface: Hard (O)

Group A 13 April Jordan defeated Qatar 2-1: Ahmed Ibrahim Ahmad Alhadid (JOR) d. Mousa Shanan Zayed (QAT) 63 61; Jabor Mohammed Ali Mutawa (QAT) d. Mohammad Al-Aisowi (JOR) 63 61; Ahmed Ibrahim Ahmad Alhadid/Fawaz El Hourani (JOR) d. Jabor Mohammed Ali Mutawa/Mousa Shanan Zayed (QAT) 75 64. **Kyrgyzstan defeated Bahrain 2-1:** Hasan Abdul-Nabi (BRN) d. Denis Surotin (KGZ) 36 63 64; Daniiar Duldaev (KGZ) d. Khaled Al Thawadi (BRN) 62 60; Daniiar Duldaev/Denis Surotin (KGZ) d. Hasan Abdul-Nabi/Khaled Al Thawadi (BRN) 61 76(5).

14 April Kyrgyzstan defeated Jordan 2-1: Ahmed Ibrahim Ahmad Alhadid (JOR) d. Evgeniy Babak (KGZ) 63 62; Daniiar Duldaev (KGZ) d. Mohammad Al-Aisowi (JOR) 62 75; Daniiar Duldaev/Denis Surotin (KGZ) d. Ahmed Ibrahim Ahmad Alhadid/Fawaz El Hourani (JOR) 62 75. **Bahrain defeated Qatar 2-1:** Mousa Shanan Zayed (QAT) d. Hasan Abdul-Nabi (BRN) 75 62; Khaled Al Thawadi (BRN) d. Jabor Mohammed Ali Mutawa (QAT) 67(4) 61 61; Hasan Abdul-Nabi/Khaled Al Thawadi (BRN) d. Mubarak Zaid/Mousa Shanan Zayed (QAT) 63 64.

15 April Jordan defeated Bahrain 3-0: Fawaz El Hourani (JOR) d. Hasan Abdul-Nabi (BRN) 46 62 60; Mohammad Al-Aisowi (JOR) d. Khaled Al Thawadi (BRN) 62 61; Ahmed Ibrahim Ahmad Alhadid/Fawaz El Hourani (JOR) d. Sayed Hazem Almoosawi/Yusuf Ebrahim Ahmed Abdulla Qaed (BRN) 60 64. **Kyrgyzstan defeated Qatar 2-1:** Mousa Shanan Zayed (QAT) d. Evgeniy Babak (KGZ) 64 20 ret.; Daniiar Duldaev (KGZ) d. Jabor Mohammed Ali Mutawa (QAT) 61 61; Daniiar Duldaev/Denis Surotin (KGZ) d. Jabor Mohammed Ali Mutawa/Mousa Shanan Zayed (QAT) 76(2) 63.

Group A final positions: 1. Kyrgyzstan, 2. Jordan, 3. Bahrain, 4. Qatar.

Group B 13 April Bangladesh defeated Turkmenistan 3-0: Sree-Amol Roy (BAN) d. Eziz Davletov (TKM) 76(6) 46 63; Shibu Lal (BAN) d. Jamshid Ilmuradov (TKM) 64 63; Mohammed-Alamgir Hossain/Ranjan Ram (BAN) d. Bahtiyar Atabaev/Jamshid Ilmuradov (TKM) 67(4) 60 61. **Iraq defeated Singapore 2-1:** Ali Khairi Hashim Al Mayahi (IRQ) d. Sean Lee (SIN) 61 61; Akram M. Abdalkarem Al-Saady (IRQ) d. Roy Hobbs (SIN) 63 46 64; Roy Hobbs/Sean Lee (SIN) d. Ali Khairi Hashim Al Mayahi/Maab Abdulrazaq Yaseen (IRQ) 62 67(6) 62.

14 April Bangladesh defeated Iraq 3-0: Sree-Amol Roy (BAN) d. Maab Abdulrazaq Yaseen (IRQ) 60 60; Shibu Lal (BAN) d. Ahmed Hamzah Abdulhasan (IRQ) 62 60; Mohammed-Alamgir Hossain/Ranjan Ram (BAN) d. Ali Khairi Hashim Al Mayahi/Akram M. Abdalkarem Al-Saady (IRQ) 60 36 64. **Singapore defeated Turkmenistan 2-1:** Eziz Davletov (TKM) d. Kunal Pawa (SIN) 57 62 62; Roy Hobbs (SIN) d. Jamshid Ilmuradov (TKM) 63 61; Daniel Heryanta Dewandaka/Roy Hobbs (SIN) d. Eziz Davletov/Jamshid Ilmuradov (TKM) 61 63.

15 April Bangladesh defeated Singapore 2-1: Sree-Amol Roy (BAN) d. Sean Lee (SIN) 61 62; Shibu Lal (BAN) d. Roy Hobbs (SIN) 64 43 def.; Daniel Heryanta Dewandaka/Kunal Pawa (SIN) d. Mohammed-Alamgir Hossain/Ranjan Ram (BAN) 62 63. **Iraq defeated Turkmenistan 2-1:** Ali Khairi Hashim Al Mayahi (IRQ) d. Bahtiyar Atabaev (TKM) 06 63 63; Akram M. Abdalkarem Al-Saady (IRQ) d. Eziz Davletov (TKM) 36 75 64; Rustam Bayramov/Jamshid Ilmuradov (TKM) d. Ahmed Hamzah Abdulhasan/Maab Abdulrazaq Yaseen (IRQ) 64 62.

Group B final positions: 1. Bangladesh, 2. Iraq, 3. Singapore, 4. Turkmenistan.

Play-off for 1st/4th positions:
16 April Bangladesh defeated Jordan 2-1: Sree-Amol Roy (BAN) d. Ahmed Ibrahim Ahmad Alhadid (JOR) 64 57 62; Mohammad Al-Aisowi (JOR) d. Shibu Lal (BAN) 76(6) 64; Ranjan Ram/Sree-Amol Roy (BAN) d. Mohammad Al-Aisowi/Fawaz El Hourani (JOR) 61 62. **Kyrgyzstan defeated Iraq 2-1:** Ali Khairi Hashim Al Mayahi (IRQ) d. Denis Surotin (KGZ) 63 75; Daniiar Duldaev (KGZ) d. Akram M. Abdalkarem Al-Saady (IRQ) 62 62; Daniiar Duldaev/Denis Surotin (KGZ) d. Ali Khairi Hashim Al Mayahi/Akram M. Abdalkarem Al-Saady (IRQ) 62 61.

Play-off for 5th/8th positions:
16 April Singapore defeated Bahrain 2-1: Sayed Hazem Almoosawi (BRN) d. Kunal Pawa (SIN) 36 30 ret.; Roy Hobbs (SIN) d. Yusuf Ebrahim Ahmed Abdulla Qaed (BRN) 61 61; Roy Hobbs/Sean Lee (SIN) d. Sayed Hazem Almoosawi/Yusuf Ebrahim Ahmed Abdulla Qaed (BRN) 26 61 61. **Qatar defeated Turkmenistan 2-0:** Mousa Shanan Zayed (QAT) d. Eziz Davletov (TKM) 21 ret.; Jabor Mohammed Ali Mutawa (QAT) d. Jamshid Ilmuradov (TKM) 10 ret.; doubles not played.

Final positions: 1=. Bangladesh, Kyrgyzstan, 3=. Iraq, Jordan, 5. Singapore, 6. Bahrain, 7. Qatar, 8. Turkmenistan.

Bangladesh and Kyrgyzstan promoted to Asia/Oceania Zone Group III in 2012.

Americas Zone
Date: 16-18 June
Venue: Santa Cruz, Bolivia
Surface: Clay (O)

16 June Trinidad & Tobago defeated US Virgin Islands 2-1: Kristepher Elien (ISV) d. Liam Gomez (TRI) 64 36 75; Yohansey Williams (TRI) d. Brian Oldfield (ISV) 61 60; Yohansey Williams/Vaughn Wilson (TRI) d. Nicholas Bass/Kristepher Elien (ISV) 61 64.

17 June Panama defeated US Virgin Islands 2-1: Carlos Silva (PAN) d. Kristepher Elien (ISV) 75 64; Alberto Gonzalez (PAN) d. Brian Oldfield (ISV) 63 60; Nicholas Bass/Kristepher Elien (ISV) d. Juan-Jose Fuentes/John Silva (PAN) 64 64.

18 June Trinidad & Tobago defeated Panama 2-1: Vaughn Wilson (TRI) d. Juan-Jose Fuentes (PAN) 64 62; Yohansey Williams (TRI) d. Carlos Silva (PAN) 63 62; Carlos Silva/John Silva (PAN) d. Yohansey Williams/Vaughn Wilson (TRI) 64 67(5) 75.

Final positions: 1. Trinidad & Tobago, 2. Panama, 3. US Virgin Islands.

Trinidad & Tobago and Panama promoted to Americas Zone Group III in 2012.

Acknowledgements

As ever, it has been a privilege to cover Davis Cup, to be present when some of the greatest players the game has ever known are making history, watching their trials and tribulations at close hand. In this cynical day and age, Davis Cup is one sports event that has maintained much of its purity: in this competition the pleasure of playing really does exceed all else. As for the winning, it's hard to imagine any player being more overjoyed than Rafael Nadal was in steering Spain to its fifth title in Seville.

After winning ten grand slam titles and two Davis Cup titles, Nadal could be expected to act a little blasé about such success, but his joy was as unconfined as it was seven years earlier in the same Olympic Stadium arena when he won the Davis Cup for the first time as an eighteen-year-old, playing in his first live rubber.

It's that sense of team spirit, of sharing, that appealed to him and his teammates, just as it does to all sportsmen and -women, but particularly professional tennis players, who mainly lead an isolated, nomadic life on tour. There is nothing quite like it anywhere else in the sport, as players soon realize once they have left it.

A Davis Cup player's success is largely dependent upon others. No matter how good a player is, he cannot do it alone. As David Nalbandian remarked, if a touch flippantly, during the final, "I would have liked to play the five matches, but I can't due to the regulations." The same goes for a Davis Cup Yearbook author. As much as he would like, it's impossible to be at more than one tie at the same time.

Consequently, one is heavily dependent upon the help of others, and I have received much, firstly from Ed Pearson, the editor, who made sure I served up the copy on time and provided invaluable help on the choice of captains for the book's new feature series.

My other thanks go to the rest of the International Tennis Federation communications team of Barbara Travers, Nick Imison, Jo Burnham, Emily Forder-White, Mitzi Ingram-Evans, Emily Bevan, Chris Archer, Monica Escolar Rojo, and Manuel Brocos; our featured captains Neale Fraser, Patrick McEnroe, Shamil Tarpischev, and Niki Pilic; and finally, for their input from World Group matches around the world, Chris Bowers, Craig Gabriel, Sandra Harwitt, Zoran Milosavljevic, Lee Goodall, Alexandra Willis, Maximiliano Boso, Richard Fleming, Neven Berticevic, Eli Weinstein, and all the players and captains of Davis Cup teams everywhere. Special thanks go to my wife, Mariola, who, not just because of her nationality, particularly enjoyed Rafa's triumph in Seville, and my three children, Chloe, Phoebe, and Elliot, for talking about little else than tennis during the past year.

Clive White

Photography Credits

- **Ron Angle** 26, 27, 28, 29, 46 (top right), 66 (bottom right)
- **Bildbyran** 23, 24, 25, 47 (middle right)
- **Sergio Carmona** 30, 31, 32
- **Maximiliano Failla** 66 (middle right), 83 (bottom left), 89, 90
- **Arne Forsell** 54, 55, 56
- **GEPA** 14-15, 16, 17, 18, 19, 83 (top right)
- **Robert Ghement** 98 (all except bottom left), 99, 102 (top left)
- **Andrei Golovanov** 94, 95 (all except far right), 96
- **Imagellan** 47 (bottom right), 82 (top left), 95 (far right)
- **Nir Keidar** 91, 92 (all except top right)
- **Halden Krog** 92 (top right), 93
- **Sergio Llamera** endpapers (front and back), 40, 41, 42, 43, 47 (bottom left), 57, 58, 59, 104-105, 106, 107 (top), 110 (top), 118 (top right and middle left)
- **Daniel Maurer/Zimmer** 33, 34, 35, 36, 67 (bottom left)
- **Susan Mullane** 47 (top left), 48-49, 50, 51, 52, 53, 103 (top right and bottom left)
- **Press Association Images** 80
- **SMP Images** 46 (bottom right), 47 (top right), 67 (top right), 82 (bottom right), 84-85, 86, 87, 88, 103 (top left and bottom right)
- **Srdjan Stevanovic** 20, 21, 22, 46 (top left), 65, 66 (top left and top right), 67 (top left), 75, 76, 77, 78, 79, 81, 82 (top right and bottom left), 102 (bottom left)
- **Takeo Tanuma** 97, 98 (bottom left), 102 (bottom right)
- **Tennis Australia** 81
- **Paul Zimmer** 5, 6, 9, 11, 12, 37, 38, 39, 46 (middle left and bottom left), 60, 61, 62, 63, 64, 66 (bottom left), 67 (bottom right), 68-69, 70, 71, 72, 73, 74, 80, 83 (top left and bottom right), 100, 101, 102 (top right), 107 (bottom), 108, 109, 110 (bottom), 111, 112, 113, 114, 115, 116, 118, 119 (top left, bottom left and bottom right)

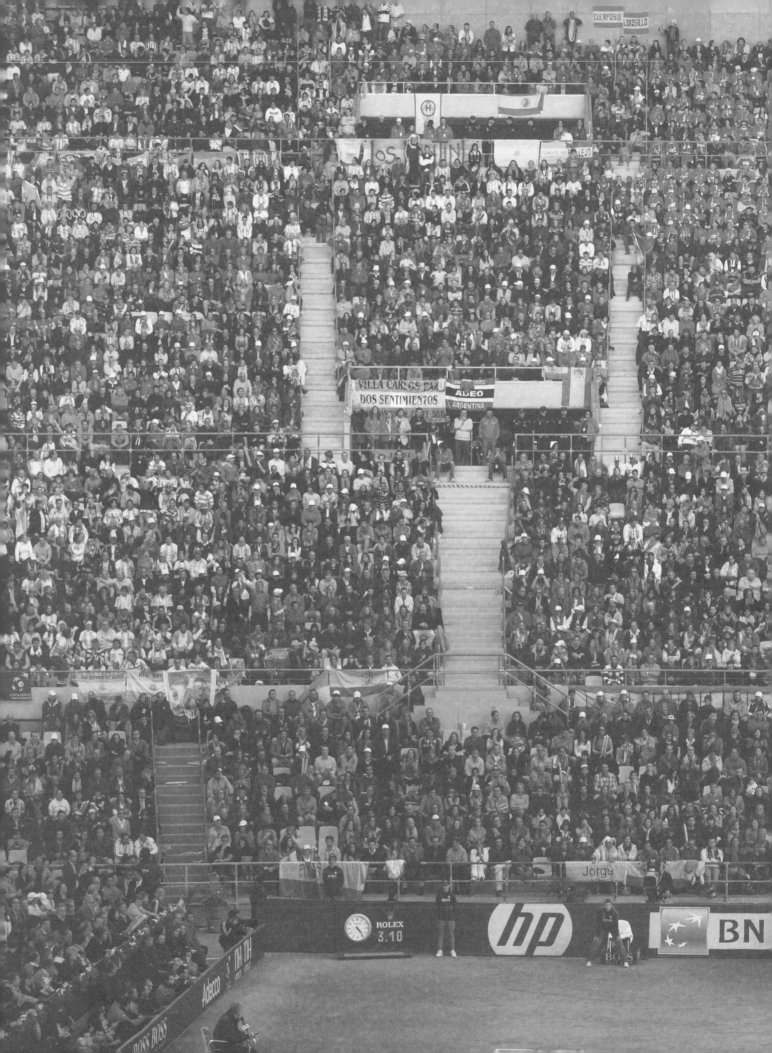